HELP TEACHERS ENGAGE STUDENTS

Action Tools for Administrat

ANNETTE BRINKMAN GARY FORLINI ELLEN WILLIAMS

EYE ON EDUCATION
6 DEPOT WAYWEST, SUITE 106
LARCHMONT, NY 10538
(914) 833–0551
(914) 833–0761 fax
www.eyeoneducation.com

Library of Congress Cataloging-in-Publication Data

Brinkman, Annette.
Help teachers engage students : action tools for administrators / Annette Brinkman, Gary Forlini, and Ellen Williams.
p. cm.
ISBN 978-1-59667-116-4
1. Teachers--In-service training. 2. School supervision. 3. Teacher-administrator relationships. 4. Motivation in education. 5. Communication in education. I. Forlini, Gary. II. Williams, Ellen, 1944- III. Title.
LB1731.B7248 2009
371.2'03--dc22
2009005709

10 9 8 7 6 5 4 3

Production services provided by
Rick Soldin, Electronic Publishing Services, Inc.
Jonesborough, TN — www.epsinc-tn.com

Also Available from Eye On Education

The Principalship from A to Z
Ron Williamson and Barbara R. Blackburn

The Instructional Leader's Guide to Informal Classroom Observations, Second Edition
Sally J. Zepeda

The Principal As Instructional Leader, Second Edition
Sally J. Zepeda

Professional Learning Communities: An Implementation Guide and Toolkit
Kathleen A. Foord and Jean M. Haar

Professional Development: What Works
Sally J. Zepeda

Motivating & Inspiring Teachers, Second Edition
Todd Whitaker, Beth Whitaker and Dale Lumpa

Get Organized! Time Management for School Leaders
Frank Buck

Creating School Cultures that Embrace Learning: What Successful Leaders Do
Tony Thacker, John S. Bell and Franklin P. Schargel

From At-Risk to Academic Excellence: What Successful Leaders Do
Franklin P. Schargel, Tony Thacker and John S. Bell

Applying Servant Leadership in Today's Schools
Mary K. Culver

Improving Your Daily Practice: A Guide for Effective School Leadership
Timothy B. Berkey

Improving Your School One Week at a Time: Building the Foundation for Professional Teaching and Learning
Jeffrey Zoul

Lead with Me: A Principal's Guide to Teacher Leadership
Gayle Moller and Anita Pankake

High Impact Leadership for High Impact Schools: The Actions that Matter Most
Pamela Salazar

Free Downloads

The tools in the Appendix of this book are available on Eye On Education's website as Adobe Acrobat files. Permission has been granted to purchasers of the book to download these tools and print them.

You can access these downloads by visiting Eye On Education's website, **www.eyeoneducation.com**, and clicking on **Free Downloads**.

You'll need your bookbuyer access code: HLP-7116–4

List of Downloads

Contents

Meet the Authors

This author team works separately and together to present and consult about classroom management and student engagement. More about their work and availability can be found at www.brinkman-forlini-williams.com or www.student-engagement.net

Annette Brinkman

Annette began her career as a classroom teacher and then a literacy specialist before becoming Utah's first Early Childhood Specialist. She then moved into school administration where she served as principal of Geneva Elementary in Utah's Alpine School District and took special interest in developing best practices in the classroom. To put her evolving techniques into wider practice, Annette moved into full-time site-based staff development in Utah's Nebo School District. It was there that Annette began to hone many of the coaching and consulting tools found in this book as principals in a variety of districts looked to her for guidance in working with new and struggling teachers. In 2006 Annette moved into the position of Associate Director in the Teaching and Learning Department of Utah's Granite School District and continues to develop techniques for coaching and consulting. She is forever grateful to her children Tyson and Tawny for their patience with her devotion to her work.

Gary Forlini

Books by Gary Forlini have been staples of classroom instruction and teacher preparation for thirty years. Beginning with the publication of ***SAT Home Study*** in 1979, Gary wrote the ***Prentice-Hall Grammar and Composition*** series and later co-authored Pearson's ***Communication in Action*** series for grades 6-12. Gary began his career as a teacher in public schools and college and later established ***Publisher's Research, Inc.*** to help private sector companies test and develop educational works for children and adults. In 1992, Gary established ***Research in Media, Inc.*** to help non-profit and for-profit organizations analyze learning dynamics and best-practices in instruction. Along the way, Gary has authored countless analytics and white papers relating to education in nearly every content area from pre-K to post-secondary, and he gratefully credits thousands of teachers and administrators who have shared their data and insights with him. He is currently working on his second novel.

Ellen Willliams

Ellen, too, began her career as a classroom teacher (20 years) and then as elementary principal (7 years) and central office administrator (5 years) before moving to Brigham Young University's department of Educational Leadership and Foundations where she co-directs two programs: Leadership Preparation and the BYU Principals Academy. Ellen's work and her publications focus on two areas for improving schools: Assessing the culture of professional learning communities (PLCs) and instructional leadership. She is co-author of ***You Can Control Your Classroom*** and has published in such scholarly journals as *Mentoring and Tutoring: A Partnership in Learning, Education and Urban Society, UCEA Journal of Case Studies, The Researcher,* and *The International Journal of Leadership in Education.* Ellen and colleagues are pioneering the development and validation of the Learning Community Culture Indicator (LCCI) to assess the presence of research-based elements found in PLCs.

The Big Eight

The heart of this book is The Big Eight, the engagement skills that your teachers need to move students forward successfully.

1	**Expectations**	Teacher ensures that students know what to do and when and how to do it.
2	**Attention Prompts**	Teacher uses verbal or visual prompts to focus students' attention for instruction to follow.
3	**Proximity**	Teacher moves purposefully around the classroom for maximum effect.
4	**Cueing**	Teacher uses positive, clear, and effective verbal Cues to clarify, maintain, or redirect activity.
5	**Signals**	Teacher employs Signals to give students ways of showing kinesthetically when they have completed a short task and are ready for the next step.
6	**Time Limits**	Teacher identifies and communicates specific times for beginning and completing tasks.
7	**Tasking**	Teacher focuses and sharpens students' engagement through questioning strategies, purposeful and thought-provoking activities, and other tactics to direct their learning.
8	**Voice**	Teacher uses Voice to maximum effect: e.g., pitch in the lower registers, tone geared for situations, diction appropriate to students' age levels, and voice modulation, or cadence, to maintain interest.

Preface and Purpose

The hope of the authors is to share roughly a combined hundred years' worth of experiences with K-12 teachers and administrators—as colleagues and friends. We consider ourselves lucky to have benefited from the lessons we've learned by listening to, observing, coaching, and mentoring the talented many serving in the trenches. In fact, our ability to identify and share The Big Eight engagement skills you will explore in this book derives directly from collecting and analyzing data from more than 500 new and struggling teachers.

Experience shows us that 80% or more of struggling teachers can become good teachers. Our greatest rewards have been the results we've seen among teachers who came to the process without the innate gifts some others enjoy, but who have consciously learned the engagement skills and strategies to such an extent that these *feel* innate to them. For these professionals, teaching has become a joy rather than a chore, and their students have become receptive, engaged learners.

Our goal in the development of this work has been to collect and distill the near-limitless possibilities for developing classroom engagement skills and to present them as a process for any administrator to adopt or adapt according to the needs of the professional staff he or she supervises—experienced teachers, new teachers, struggling teachers.

No system should be rigid or finite in its practice or possibilities, so our intent is to weave into these presentations some open-endedness to enable administrators to adapt our tools and other ideas at will—as specific needs dictate and as personal and professional styles require.

What you will find in these pages are stages and steps in a process aimed at helping every teacher develop and hone the skills necessary—The Big Eight—to engage students for optimal learning. For each engagement skill, and within each stage, we provide *tools*—specific documents: forms, charts, cards—to enable and facilitate and to record and track the progress of each staff member.

Organization of this Book

This book offers a baseline of information about essential classroom engagement skills for immersing students in learning, plus a series of steps you can follow or adapt in observing, debriefing, consulting, or coaching your teachers.

Think of this book as a guide for helping your teachers recognize and master the strategies necessary for maximizing student engagement in their learning. In this book, we focus on engagement skills and strategies because, simply enough, teachers need to use them or else kids won't learn. The Great Ones already practice engagement strategies masterfully, many through the instincts that come with being naturally gifted teachers. Good teachers have success partly because they have developed engagement strategies that have worked for them over time, yet they may yet grow more proficient as they practice and hone their skills. Who wouldn't?

New and struggling teachers, on the other hand, may be a major concern of your observations. Time spent assisting new teachers helps them avoid developing bad practices and leads them more quickly to effective student engagement. You may recognize signs of a teacher in trouble:

Warning Signs of a Teacher in Trouble

- Consistent parental complaints
- Excessive amounts of office referrals or complaints from teacher about individual students
- Chaos or loud noise coming from a classroom
- Messy, disorganized room or a room that appears barren; displays relating to grade level or subject area are not apparent
- Frequent absences for students and teacher
- Low test scores
- Apparent lack of lesson preparation; instruction that is worksheet-driven (Zepeda, 2007a)

Surely, you wish to know how to diagnose your teacher's problems or needs, what kinds of data you need to collect for diagnosing and prescribing remedies, what specific steps and strategies you might employ to help your teacher, and what tools you might use in this process. **In addition to recognizing The Big Eight engagement skills and understanding their aspects, you will find specific tools in this book that you can use to observe teachers, to focus debriefings, and to assist your teachers in discovering or developing or honing their classroom skills.**

How to Use This Book

Understanding the three major sections of this book will help you transfer the devices within into actual practice.

The first section, Chapters 1 through 3, presents a summary of the eight key engagement skills—The Big Eight—as well as an overview of the process for observing, debriefing, consulting, and coaching your teachers. If you use nothing more than the first section, you may have enough to plan and support your work. Chapter 1 provides an overview of a process for helping teachers master essential classroom skills—all in the context of accepted standards for instruction. Indeed, recognizing and understanding Instructional Standards—whether you focus on national standards, your district's, or the model we provide—should be a kind of backdrop or baseline for each teacher's classroom performance. In most districts, Instructional Standards are shared with all concerned—teachers, principals, staff developers, mentors, coaches—who have a stake in teacher excellence in the classroom.

Every administrator recognizes that steps designed to help teachers improve and excel in the classroom are not isolated events. Instead, a process providing direct assistance for teachers must be understood in its larger context. For instance, the process itself must be rooted in sound, recognizable, understandable standards for instruction. We provide an overview of these for you in Chapter 1 while incorporating well-recognized and current research, and we end Chapter 1 with an evaluation tool should you decide to inventory a teacher's performance according to district or national standards.

The second section, Chapters 3 through 11, explores The Big Eight engagement skills in greater depth with additional tools for observing, consulting, and coaching your teacher and for choosing the stances you can take to most effectively benefit your teacher. The steps in our process, we recognize, must be grounded in concrete information about how teachers engage students in positive, constructive learning as well as actionable strategies *for you* in consulting with and coaching teachers. Much of this information you will find outlined in depth in this central section of the book, where we offer you case studies of teachers' successful development of their engagement skills, as well as specific tactics you can use to lead your teacher toward greater success in the classroom.

Central to our process are the classroom *engagement skills and strategies* that you will observe and track. We call these *The Big Eight* because each of them encompasses a range of related skill-behaviors. Each skill chapter supports your process with tools and steps designed to communicate and inculcate knowledge of these behaviors. Naturally, the goal of everyone involved will be to maximize teacher performance using all eight engagement skills, with the understanding that some teachers may need to focus on ones you deem most critical for them to develop or sharpen so they can achieve greater success, the result being higher student achievement—the ultimate and most desirable outcome.

You most likely are no stranger to teacher observations and debriefings. As you learn more about The Big Eight, and as you focus your process for observing and communicating with your teachers, you may find that certain tools will facilitate communication while helping you further develop constructive relationships with your teachers. **Throughout, we will invite you to utilize our tools and routines or to modify them as you see fit.**

It is our hope that Chapters 3 through 11 will sharpen your own recognition of these eight essential engagement skills so that you can collect and track data about them while building your teachers' own meta-cognitive awareness, ultimately enabling your teachers to develop or sharpen these skills independently and in an ongoing manner.

The third section, Chapter 12, revisits the larger context in which our process—and yours—must be understood. In short, the process of helping teachers master the skills they need to succeed in the classroom must be viewed as part of a larger picture of their performance and contributions to your entire community of learners. Our final chapter, then, places the process in context with the five recognized Domains of Teacher Performance: Instruction, Environment, Profession, Assessment, and Community.

Throughout this book, from Chapter 1 to 12, you may find that the tools we provide—in context and in our Appendix—can serve as the workhorses of your own process. In most instances where we introduce a tool in the context of an engagement skill, we provide a partially- or fully-completed model of the tool to discuss ways in which you can use it. **Equally important, to assist and facilitate your process, we offer you all tools packed in a logical sequence in the Appendix to this book so that you can reproduce them at will and as needed.**

1

Recognizing Performance Standards

Everyone wants teachers to succeed. Despite the obvious truth that districts cannot afford high levels of teacher failure, administrators recognize they have a moral obligation to help teachers and to give them all the support possible. Ultimately, children respond and learn best in a culture of support and achievement.

Active involvement in building teachers' skills helps build a positive culture within a school—a culture of trust. In an 18–month study of teacher turnovers, Barnes, Crowe, and Shaefer (2003) found that every teacher job turnover costs a district $1,500 or more per teacher for the training, rehiring, and record keeping that had been involved. **Looking at small and large districts, the study found that the costs of teacher turnover—recruiting, hiring, and training—are substantial.** Barnes, et al. (2003) cite numerous examples: In Granville County, North Carolina, for instance, the cost of each teacher who left the district was just under $10,000. In a small rural district such as Jemez Valley, New Mexico, the cost per teacher was $4,366. In Milwaukee, the average cost per teacher-leaver was $15,325. In a very large district like Chicago, the average cost was $17,872 per leaver. The total cost of turnover in the Chicago Public Schools is estimated to be more than $86 million per year. It is clear that thousands of dollars walk out the door each time a teacher leaves (Gary Barnes, Ph.D., Benjamin Schaefer, National Commission on Teaching and America's Future).

Performance Standards: Four Domains for Evaluation

Surely, we are not the first to codify the practices of good instruction, nor will we be the last. Most school districts have developed their own standards, or domains, for classroom instruction, which become benchmarks for formal and informal observations that every building administrator conducts on a regular basis. Many, perhaps most, of these local standards derive from or resemble national standards, so it makes sense for us to begin with these.

With the kind permission of the Granite School District in Utah, we use their standards as we discuss teacher performance requirements (Granite School District, 2006). Granite's standards of teacher performance not only reflect published national standards such as *The Five Core Propositions* set forth by the National Board for Professional Teaching

Standards (1987) and the work of Charlotte Danielson (1996, 2000), a former teacher and administrator who consults on teacher quality and evaluation, they result also from a three-year collaborative process in which a committee of administrators, teachers, and union representatives piloted and consulted and fine-tuned this body of work.

Standards like these help frame for you what effective, successful teaching practice entails—in essence, what an effective teacher practices. While you already know all or most of this—by instinct and/or through experience—it's useful to review these to maintain a complete and objective view of teacher performance.

Domain I. In most districts, Domain I captures the essential elements of instruction and assessment. **This domain represents how teachers interact with students to promote, produce, and assess learning:**

Domain I: Instruction and Assessment

A. The educator consistently communicates clearly and accurately.

B. The educator uses a variety of effective instructional strategies.

C. The educator uses a variety of engagement strategies.

D. The educator involves students and/or staff in meaningful learning.

E. The educator makes reasonable and appropriate individual accommodations.

F. The educator uses assessment to guide instruction and verify that meaningful learning is taking place.

G. The educator systematically reviews and reinforces concepts to support long-term learning (Granite School District, 2006).

Domain II. Planning and preparation are vital to a productive classroom culture. Before any successful educator stands before a class, he or she will have spent substantial time planning and organizing materials for lessons that are based on the differentiated needs of students. And this teacher will have developed and accessed data that help inform differentiation. **Domain II captures the essential ingredients of planning and preparation:**

Domain II: Planning and Preparation

A. The educator uses appropriate curriculum materials in planning for instruction.

B. The educator plans and prepares for the needs of diverse learners.

C. The educator sets goals and makes instructional decisions based on data gathered from multiple sources.

D. The educator applies knowledge of developmentally appropriate practices when planning instruction.

E. The educator collaborates with colleagues in planning instruction, effectively using resources, and providing support (Granite School District, 2006).

Domain III. Educators who create an environment conducive to learning increase the likelihood that students will thrive. Marilyn Jageur Adams (1997), noted brain researcher, has observed "the brain learns in direct proportion to its emotional security," and so **it is critical that every successful teacher develop strategies for creating and maintaining an environment that encourages children to explore the subjects at hand and to feel secure doing so.**

Teachers who are unable to nurture and sustain a culture for learning often create uncertainty and develop negative relationships with students due to their lack of consistency and their failure to communicate in positive, constructive ways. Without effective classroom management routines and techniques in place, optimal learning cannot and does not occur.

Domain III is the focus of this book because a struggling teacher will most likely be deficient in this domain, and so your attention to Domain III will be critical in working with and assisting that teacher:

Domain III: Learning Environment

A. The educator shows and elicits respect while developing and maintaining positive rapport.

B. The educator supports colleagues.

C. The educator advocates, nurtures, and sustains a culture for learning.

D. The educator manages procedures.

E. The educator manages student behavior.

F. The educator prepares and maintains an environment conducive to learning (Granite School District, 2006).

Domain IV. Domain IV captures the essential responsibilities of participating positively in a community of professionals:

Domain IV: Professional Responsibilities

A. The educator participates in professional growth.

B. The educator interacts and communicates with all constituency groups.

C. The educator maintains professional appearance and behavior.

D. The educator performs necessary noninstructional duties.

E. The educator demonstrates professional leadership (Granite School District, 2006).

Focusing on Domain III

The responsibility of the principal is to be alert to the aspects of Domain III and to consider every teacher in regards to the standards of this domain. **Domain III is the principal focus of this book along with domains I and II because these domains have the most direct impact on students' lives and on their learning. Those impacts are tangible and measurable.**

When teachers are ineffective classroom managers, you can expect students' learning to suffer. As an observer in such a classroom, you may notice that students appear confused or simply disengaged, and you may feel that the classroom environment somehow doesn't support positive interactions. You may even think the environment feels negative.

You may decide to take stock of a teacher's standing in regards to the specific standards in Domain III. You may recognize certain conditions like the ones we have discovered during our observations, which lead you to focus on this domain. These are a few:

- Chaos and disorganization in the classroom
- Children referred by this teacher for bad behavior or, worse, who are injured in this classroom
- Parental complaints including requests for transfers out of this class
- Complaints from this teacher's colleagues regarding noise and other kinds of disruptions that travel from that classroom to other locations within the school
- Higher absenteeism among this teacher's students
- High percentages of students failing or scoring poorly in this class
- Poor results of this teacher's students on standardized testing
- Adversarial relationships between this teacher and individual students

The tool on the facing page, offered as a reproducible in the Appendix (p. 152), presents the specific elements of the Domain III standards according to a range of possible behaviors from "Above Standard," which would receive a 3 on the Rubric to "Below Standard," which would receive 0 (Granite School District, 2005).

Domain III: Standards and Rubric for Learning Environment

Standard	ABOVE STANDARD (3)	MEETS STANDARD (2)	APPROACHES STANDARD (1)	BELOW STANDARD (0)	SCORE
LEARNING ENVIRONMENT—DOMAIN III					
A. The educator shows and elicits respect while developing and maintaining positive rapport.	• Fosters a safe/ equitable learning community. • Facilitates student participation in creating a climate of equity and respect.	• Facilitates a caring and motivating environment. • Encourages positive social interaction. • Promotes cooperative and collaborative learning.	• Builds rapport with most students. • Models respectful relationships. • Utilizes some strategies to respond to disrespect.	• Disrespect is exhibited by teacher and students. • Rules are inconsistent.	
B. The educator advocates, nurtures, and sustains a culture for learning.	• Encourages students to set personal goals and high expectations. • Designs movement patterns and access to resources to promote engagement.	• Sets and maintains high expectations. • Develops self-motivation and active engagement in learning. • Recognizes the importance of establishing a climate of learning.	• Develops some expectations. • Applies engagement strategies. • Provides opportunities for group interaction.	• Inconsistent or low Expectations. • No Expectations for students to engage in their own learning or to work with peers.	
C. The educator manages procedures.	• Assists all students in developing and internalizing equitable routines, procedures, and habits. • Facilitates student ownership of classroom habits and procedures.	• Arranges and directs procedures with minimum disruption. • Manages transitions effectively. • Maximizes the amount of time spent in learning. • Applies procedures and enforces rules consistently.	• Establishes some procedures and classroom rules to support student learning. • Develops student awareness of the procedures. • Spends the majority of structured time learning (e.g., reading, content focus).	• Minimal or no classroom rules or procedures are evident. • Teacher directions and procedures are confusing. • Instructional time is lost during transitions.	
D. The educator manages student behavior.	• Presents, adjusts, and facilitates instruction and daily activities so students are engaged. • Facilitates student problem solving of interpersonal conflicts.	• Explains rules, expectations, and consequences. • Explains reasons for disciplinary actions. • Administers discipline that fits the infraction in a calm, professional demeanor. • Uses fair and consistent practices.	• Communicates rules and consequences. • Responds to disruptive behavior. • Develops some routines for classroom procedures.	• Rules are not defined or communicated to students. • Discipline is inconsistent and does not correlate to the infraction.	
E. The educator prepares and maintains an environment conducive to learning	• Uses the physical environment to promote individual and group learning.	• Designs movement and resources to promote individual and group engagement. • Uses room displays in learning activities.	• Manages room for easy movement and access to resources. • Uses room displays that represent current topics of study.	• Movement patterns are awkward.	

Reproducible: Page 152, Appendix

2

Diagnosing and Prescribing

Every school has teachers who struggle in their efforts to ensure that children learn to the best of their abilities. Some struggling teachers achieve limited success; others virtually no success at all. And we know that schools failing to address the needs of struggling teachers are schools where morale may be flagging, where students are underperforming, and where learning generally is not rising to levels that all desire (Zepeda, 2007a).

Every school—even failing schools—has administrators who know or sense where challenges exist and who wish to provide assistance to all—especially to those in most serious trouble. Too often, however, school administrators undertreat struggling teachers because they don't have the tools or do not know how to diagnose specific problems, nor do they have access to the remedies that just might work (Zepeda, 2007a). It is often true that most principals were good teachers themselves and achieved significant successes in managing their own classrooms. Perhaps they consciously developed the tactics and strategies that led to their instructional successes, or perhaps they came to the profession naturally—unconsciously competent, let's say—rich in the instincts that make teachers successful and help them grow ever better.

Administrators who were competent teachers sometimes find it difficult to spot the specific elements of a teacher's struggle because they themselves never struggled with the same or similar problems. In effect, some administrators are too far removed from the problems that some of their teachers face. They may spot a problem but feel unsure about the remedy.

Until you as an administrator can consciously label and define what may be going wrong systemically in any given classroom, you may see the symptoms—many of them subtle; others glaring or too numerous—but you may miss the root problems that need to be addressed head on.

This chapter will help you close the gap between your teachers in need and the skills you can bring to bear to help them. For instance, you can't simply tell a teacher to get more students on task; you must first recognize the failures in the instructional dynamics that are leading to off-task behavior, and then you must lead that teacher toward recognizing and discovering, or honing, the tactics and strategies that will work. Specifically, this chapter offers you the following elements:

- A brief, thumbnail overview of the **eight engagement skills** (The Big Eight) that your teachers need to use and use well
- Tools for **preliminary classroom observations**
- Guidelines for making **initial diagnoses** and
- Tools for **follow-up observations** that will lead to **focused consultations** with your teachers.

Concentrate on Engagement Skills!

In most instances, you probably will embark on a classroom observation with some foreknowledge of your teacher's level of classroom experience and expertise. In other instances, you may encounter a teacher who is new—or new to you. Naturally, when you evaluate to determine what, if anything, your teacher needs to focus on and develop, you will remain cognizant of the relevant performance standards (e.g., those outlined in Chapter 1). **More specifically, as you make your initial classroom observations, you will want to get to the core of any problems that may exist, and the key to unlocking this core is in recognizing the eight major engagement skills (The Big Eight). Keep your eye on these in particular.**

In every instance when your teacher communicates, directs, and otherwise interacts with students, the rubber meets the road, figuratively. These are the flashpoints you should observe, and by recognizing The Big Eight engagement skills, you will have specific elements to identify and measure using specific tools for observation and assistance.

You may decide to focus on all eight engagement skills for one teacher, or only one with another, or a combination of skills with yet other teachers. The individual skill chapters that follow (Chapters 4 to 11) are organized to encourage working with teachers on more than one skill through the improvement process, and they contain tools to facilitate your process. Let teachers' needs dictate the number of skills you address over time.

The chart on the facing page outlines and defines The Big Eight and their bases in research.

The Big Eight Engagement Skills for Instruction		
1	**Expectations**	**Teacher ensures that students know what to do and when and how to do it** (Colvin, Sugai, Good, and Lee, 1997, Lane, Webby, and Menzies, 2003; Lo, Loe, and Cartledge, 2002).
2	**Attention Prompts**	**Teacher uses verbal or visual prompts to focus students' Attention for instruction to follow** (Carnine, Silbert, Kame'enui, & Tarver, 2004).
3	**Proximity**	**Teacher moves purposefully around the classroom for maximum effect** (De Pry & Sugai, 2002; Johnson, Stoner, & Green, 1996).
4	**Cueing**	**Teacher uses positive, clear, and effective verbal Cues to clarify, maintain, or redirect activity** (Alberto and Troutman, 2006; Cooper, Heron, and Heward, 2007; Ferguson and Houghton, 1992).
5	**Signals**	**Teacher employs Signals to give students ways of showing kinesthetically when they have completed a short task and are ready for the next step** (Becker and Gersten, 1982).
6	**Time Limits**	**Teacher identifies and communicates specific times for beginning and completing tasks.**
7	**Tasking**	**Teacher focuses and sharpens students' engagement through questioning strategies, purposeful and thought-provoking activities, and other tactics to direct their learning** (Carnine, Silbert, Kame'enui, and Tarver, 2004; Godfrey, Grisham-Brown, and Schuster, 2003; Greenwood, Horton, and Utley, 2002; Sutherland, Alder, and Gunter, 2003).
8	**Voice**	**Teacher uses Voice to maximum effect: e.g., pitch in the lower registers, tone geared for situations, diction appropriate to students' age levels, and voice modulation, or cadence, to maintain interest** (Anderson, 1961).

The primary purpose of the tools in each chapter is to support your process of collecting data your teachers need in order to grow more effective and to maximize student engagement. Following are descriptions of the major tools. These will help you start with observations and evaluations and then follow through with direct assistance:

The Major Tools for Evaluation and Assistance	
Tool	**Type and Purpose**
Drop-In Tool	**Quick (5 minute) checkup on classroom management**. This tool also utilizes a "Leave Behind" card to give the teacher immediate feedback on his/her keepers and one item to polish.
Time-on-Task Tool	**Diagnostic data collection tool to quickly (15 to 20 minutes) collect classroom management (engagement) data for an individual teacher.** The tool is organized so that you can easily determine a starting place to maximize teacher growth.
Focused Observation Tool	**Skill-focused data collection tool, one for each of The Big Eight engagement strategies:** Expectations, Attention Prompts, Proximity, Cueing, Signals, Time Limits, Tasking, and Voice. Each tool is specific to one engagement skill and requires a 15–minute observation.
Depth Observation Tool	**Tool for in-depth understanding of an engagement skill**. Each tool develops more focused data for each skill and requires a 20– to 30– minute observation.
Demo Observation Tool	**Tool for the new and/or struggling teacher to use while observing a master demonstration teacher.** For each of The Big Eight, this tool helps you and your teacher gather specific data to model and inform instructional improvement strategies.

Know Where to Start

For your initial diagnosis of an entire staff or an individual teacher, you will use the *Drop-In Tool* and the *Time-on-Task Tool*. These are the best preliminary tools because they begin with a broad view to help you observe for, and account for, any and all of The Big Eight engagement skills. The next chart summarizes the purposes and outcomes of these two baseline tools.

Baseline Diagnostic Tools

	Drop-In Tool	**Time-on-Task Tool**
Purpose	♦ Gather engagement data about a large number of teachers in a very short amount of time.	♦ Diagnose a starting place with a teacher struggling with student engagement. ♦ Help new teachers identify focused areas for growth.
Outcome(s)	♦ Schoolwide data that shows patterns of strengths and weaknesses that can be utilized to plan professional development. ♦ Teacher-specific data to use for engaging teachers in a dialogue to look for patterns of strengths and to identify areas for refinements. ♦ Regular feedback for all teachers that highlight strengths and areas for refinement.	♦ Data that can be used to identify an aspect of engagement that teachers can focus on to expedite their growth and success. ♦ Specific data that can be used to accelerate the learning curve of new teachers.
Audience	♦ ALL teachers.	♦ Struggling teachers. ♦ New teachers.
Time Commitment	♦ Goal is one grade level per day three days per week. ♦ Each Drop-In takes 5 minutes.	♦ 20–minute observation. ♦ With struggling teachers this should occur on a monthly basis for reevaluation of next focus. ♦ New teachers during first month of the school year.
Stance	♦ Mentor: Consultant or Coach.	♦ Consultant or Evaluator.

Use *Drop-In Tools* Early!

We recommend informal Drop-Ins early in the school year, perhaps during the first few weeks of the first semester. You might conduct Drop-Ins for all teachers, for one team at a time, or for teachers you already have identified needing support.

Think of a Drop-In as an informal, first-blush, balcony-view observation. Its purpose is to take an initial pulse-reading, an opportunity to begin collecting data and to begin identifying strengths, weaknesses, or problematic issues to address going forward.

While arguably the most important component of student engagement is the student himself or herself, the teacher brings to the immediate task two very important elements:

- **Physical Environment:** aspects of the classroom setting that foster interest and support learning, and
- **Engagement Skills:** specific tactics and strategies teachers use to encourage students to learn.

Your initial Drop-Ins should focus on the broad-spectrum of Domain III, the Learning Environment. Observe the big picture, your teacher's classroom and instruction.

Drop-In events should not be approached as peer Drop-Ins or administrator-wanderings. Instead, they should be 5–minute administrator walks for the purpose of focusing on physical environment and student engagement. **Keep in mind these DOs and DON'Ts of Drop-Ins:**

Drop-In Tool

Name: *Mr. Blair Smith* Date/Time: *9/15/08, 9:00am*
Grade/Subject: *5th grade/math* Observer: *Tim Jones*

Rating System:

✓+ = Strategy exceptionally well done
✓– = Strategy attempted, not effective
✓ = Strategy apparent and competent
– = Strategy missing, should occur

Physical Environment: (Domain III. Learning Environment):

- *✓* Student work is on display and clearly demonstrates the objective
- *✓–* Student Expectations for behavior are posted
- *✓–* Room is organized with easy access to materials
- *✓–* Room arrangement lends itself to physical movement
- *✓* Learning objective is posted
- *✓* Schedule is posted

Classroom Management/Engagement: (Domain III. Learning Environment):

- *–* Students know what to do and when and how to do it (EXPECTATIONS)
- *✓* Teacher uses prompts to focus instruction to follow (ATTENTION)
- *✓+* Teacher moves purposefully around the classroom (PROXIMITY)
- *–* Teacher uses positive, effective verbal Cues (CUEING)
- *–* Teacher uses nonverbal Signals to direct students (SIGNALS)
- *–* Teacher offers times for beginning and ending tasks (TIME LIMITS)
- *✓–* Teacher sharpens engagement through questioning strategies (TASKING)
- *✓–* Teacher uses positive, clear, effective tone and verbiage (VOICE)

Student Engagement: (Domain III. Learning Environment): 25 # students

Approximate PERCENTAGE of student engagement: *30-50%*

Students are engaged in work directly related to the objective. *✓* YES ___ NO

Comments/Questions: *Excellent use of Proximity. Lack of Signals from students.*

Follow-Up: *Do a 20-minute engagement observation. Watch for lack of Cueing and Expectations.*

Reproducible: Page 153, Appendix

A Drop-In **Is** . . .	A Drop-In **Is Not** . . .
♦ A way to see the "big picture" ♦ A way to visit several teachers in a short period of time ♦ A way to begin developing data-based needs assessment	♦ An evaluation ♦ A formal visit ♦ A time to converse with a teacher about problems ♦ LONG!!!

Normally, it is a good idea to let your teachers know that you will be conducting 5–minute Drop-Ins and to explain that these visits will focus on engagement skills. You may decide to conduct Drop-Ins for every new teacher's classroom and anyone that you worry is struggling with student engagement. It is helpful to conduct Drop-Ins more than once and at different times of day before analyzing a teacher's strengths and problems.

The tool on the facing page is an example of a *Drop-In Tool* completed by a principal after visiting a 5th grade math lesson. This tool, like others, uses a simple system to rate each aspect:

✓+ = Strategy exceptionally well done!
✓ = Strategy apparent and competent.
✓– = Strategy attempted but not effective.
– = Strategy missing, should be occurring.

Follow these steps as you complete a *Drop-In Tool.*

STEP 1: As you enter the classroom, look at the physical environment and ask yourself the following questions, noting the answers on the *Physical Environment* portion of the tool:

- To what degree is student work on display that clearly demonstrates objectives?
- Are student Expectations for behavior posted and clearly obvious? Is the learning objective posted?
- Is the daily schedule of work/activity posted, clear, and obvious?
- To what degree is the room organized with easy access to materials?
- To what degree does the room lend itself to physical movement?

STEP 2: Focus your attention on the specific engagement skills, noting the answers on the *Classroom Management* portion of the tool:

- Do students know what to do, when, and how to do it? (Expectations)
- Does the teacher use Attention Prompts to focus instruction that will follow? (Attention)
- Does the teacher move purposefully around the room? (Proximity)
- Does the teacher offer positive and effective verbal Cues? (Cueing)
- Does the teacher use nonverbal Signals to direct students? (Signals)
- Has the teacher provided specific times for beginning and completing work? (Time Limits)
- Does the teacher focus and sharpen students' engagement through questioning strategies and engagement activities? (Tasking)
- Is the teacher's tone and verbiage positive, clear, and effective? (Voice)

Reflection Follow-Up

Name: *Blair Smith* Date: *9/15/08*
Grade/Subject: *5th math* Observer: *Tim Jones*

Keepers: *Using Proximity helped redirect individual students. I did appreciate seeing both your learning objective and daily schedule posted*

Polishers: *What behavioral Cues could you whisper to students while you are doing Proximity*

Reproducible: Page 154, Appendix

STEP 3: Note the approximate percentage of student engagement as well as your YES/NO perception of student engagement in the objectives of the lesson.

STEP 4: Write the engagement strategies you feel are done well under *Keepers*, and identify the strategies needing work under *Polishers*. Add a *Follow-Up* note to yourself on the *Drop-In Tool* for next steps you plan to take.

STEP 5: Leave the *Reflection Follow-Up* card with your teacher at the completion of the visit. The sample here is one the principal left with Mr. Smith following the Drop-In visit.

OTHER STEPS: Early in the process of conducting Drop-Ins—perhaps before you actually make your first visit—clarify your purposes with staff. This builds trust and buy-in:

- Announce your plan to conduct Drop-Ins and schedule a time, perhaps one day or more.
- Give teachers a Signal that they can use (e.g., a thumbs-down) if the time is not right for you to walk through.
- Emphasize the positive rather than the negative regarding your purposes (and your findings) in Drop-Ins.
- Emphasize that these will be 4– to 5–minute visits, and ask that teachers not change their plans or tactics when they see you arrive.
- Announce your intent to leave behind a *Reflection Follow-Up* card.

Remember: Drop-Ins are your first step toward diagnosis. Each Drop-In is a quick way to identify engagement problems your individual teachers may have or to identify the engagement skills that need to be addressed among several teachers—perhaps an entire team.

Follow Through with Engagement Observations

Following your initial Drop-Ins, move toward a more specific diagnosis by performing 20–minute sit-down observations using a ***Time-On-Task Tool***. Among the many advantages of a ***Time-On-Task Tool*** are its brevity and focus. That is, during a relatively brief observation of 15 to 20 minutes, you can home in on each of the specific engagement skills as you listen, observe your teacher, and watch students.

An important element of a ***Time-On-Task Tool*** is that it provides a simple structure for collecting these specific data points during time intervals within your observation:

Data You Can Collect Using a *Time-on-Task Tool*

- Percentage of students engaged in learning
- Teacher actions, or inactions, leading to student disengagement
- Relevant student behavior, particularly off-task
- Tracking or tallying of teacher's use of engagement questioning
- Needs and recommendations for attention to specific engagement strategies
- Notations of actions teacher performs well

As you use a ***Time-On-Task Tool,*** keep these two guiding principles in mind:

- Watch students and listen to the teacher. Student behavior gives you insight into certain strategies that the teacher is or is not using correctly, and
- Remain focused on *engagement*, not on the specifics of curriculum content.

Following is a completed ***Time-On-Task Tool*** used during a 15–minute visit to the 6th grade language arts class of teacher Samantha Samuels. As you scan the data about student engagement entered by the principal during each interval within the observation, note the use of the notation **A** to indicate "Active Student Behavior," meaning the percentage of students who appear constructively engaged in the lesson. Note also that the notation **P** indicates "Passive Student Behavior," meaning the percentage of students who do not appear engaged, including some who may appear unfocused or distracted as well as some who may be clearly misbehaving or otherwise off-track.

Time-On-Task (Observation Tool for All Engagement Skills)

Name: *Samantha Samuels* Date: *Oct. 15, 2009* # Students: *25* Grade/Class: *6th Grade* Observer: *Ms. Elliot*

Directions: Record the time for each observation you make of educator involvement in learning. Record observations as follows:

1. Mark percentage of student engagement. (P) passive, (A) active
2. Describe teacher actions causing disengagement.
3. Describe relevant student behavior, especially off-task behavior.
4. Ask yourself, "What would I do if I were the teacher?"
5. Check recommended action(s)—those things that you would do if you were the teacher. You may also want to ★ actions that the teacher performs well.

FOR EACH INTERVAL, show % of Student Engagement.

WRITE **A** for alert, attentive behavior, or **P** for passive, disengaged behavior. **THEN DESCRIBE**

INTERVALS	Teacher Actions Impacting Students (Below) AND Student Engagement and Behavior (Below)		RECOMMENDED ACTIONS: Expectations	Attention Prompts	Proximity	Cueing	Signals	Time Limits	Tasking	Voice
Interval No. 1 12:12 pm	% Engaged: *A* 0–5% ___ 6–25% *A* 26–33% ___ 34–50% ___ 51–79% *P* 80–100%				X X	X X			X X X	
	Teacher Actions: *Do we know ...? (open questions) Snap of fingers (social cues?) How can all students be engaged before 1 responds? ________, sit up (social cues)?*	**Student Behavior:** *1 Sleeping, 1 reading, 1 writing ono desk, w chatting (need Proximity here?)*								
Interval No. 2 12:15 pm	% Engaged: *A* 0–5% ___ 6–25% ___ 26–33% ___ 34–50% *A* 51–79% *P* 80–100%		★						X X	
	Teacher Actions: *What did he say? Is that part of the conflict? (Questioning? How can all students be engaged in response?) What event? Who is going to hurt whom?(open?)*	**Student Behavior:** *Note-taking guide 1 reading aloud*								
Interval No. 3 12:17 pm	% Engaged: ___ 0–5% *A* 6–25% ___ 26–33% ___ 34–50% *A* 51–79% *P* 80–100%				X				X X	
	Teacher Actions: *Who sounds like the bad guy? Why would he become ...? How does that mean ...? (open questions: How can all students be engaged in response)*	**Student Behavior:** *Tracking, nothing, sleeping, writing notes*								
Interval No. 4 12:21 am	% Engaged: ___ 0–5% ___ 6–25% ___ 26–33% *A* 34–50% *P* 51–79% ___ 80–100%				X X				X X	
	Teacher Actions: *Put your books away and move into your assigned groups. (Time limit?) (Signal when ready?)*	**Student Behavior:** *Some move quickly; others talking, wandering, pushing. (Cues?) (Expectations?)*								
Interval No. 5	% Engaged: ___ 0–5% ___ 6–25% ___ 26–33% ___ 34–50% ___ 51–79% ___ 80–100%									
	Teacher Actions:	**Student Behavior:**								

Recommended Actions:

Reduce number of open questions by increasing engagement questions, and start by giving method of response before asking the question.

Open questions: iiiii iiiii iiiii iiiii ii = 22

As you look closely at this ***Time-On-Task Tool***, you will notice a few more data points the principal collected for subsequent debriefing with the teacher:

- Recommendations for focusing on specific engagement strategies (the X's in the right columns)
- Notations of the engagement skills performed well (the star in the right column under Expectations.)
- Anecdotal data about specific teacher actions and resulting student behavior
- Question Tallies: The number of times the teacher asked each kind of question normally intended to keep students on task: open, assessment, and engagement questions
- A specific recommended action to be discussed at a later date.

Notice also that the ***Time-On-Task Tool*** contains a set of directions at the top to remind you about the relevant data collection procedures. If you have not used this instrument in the past or are just now becoming familiar with it, here are the directions in greater detail:

Directions for Using *Time-On-Task Tools*

1. **Record Time for Each Interval:** In the left column, write the start time (e.g., 12:12 pm) for each 3– or 4–minute segment you observe for relevant data.
2. **Note Numbers of Students Engaged during Each Interval:** Each interval has a check-off spot for approximate percentages (e.g., 0–5% or 6–25%) where you can place either a check or a more specific entry such as **A** for percentage of students exhibiting active, engaged performance, and **P** for the percentage of students who appear passive or off-task.
3. **Describe Teacher Actions during Each Interval:** For teacher actions you consider applicable to student engagement, write a word, brief phrase, or sentence that captures what you hear the teacher doing and saying.
4. **Describe Relevant Student Actions:** Write the concrete facts, not opinions, of what you see students doing, or not doing, during the interval. Pay special attention to off-task behavior.
5. **Place an X Next to the Strategies You Recommend:** This is key. For each interval where you spot student disengagement, ask yourself "What would I be doing if I were the teacher?" Then place an X in the appropriate strategy column to indicate the strategy your teacher should have utilized. For instance, if you think the teacher should have moved closer to the two boys playing tic-tac-toe quietly, you might place an X in the ***Proximity*** column. (Note: You might also STAR whichever strategies you think your teacher is using effectively.)
6. **Tally the Kinds of Questions You Hear:** At the bottom of this tool under "Recommended Actions," you might tick off each kind of question you find problematic,

such as too many "open questions." (The chapter on Tasking will help train your ears for each kind of question.) This will help you create baseline data of the pattern of questioning your teacher uses, because a teacher's expertise in formulating the right kinds of questions is fundamental to engaging students constructively. For now, before you get to our Tasking chapter, use this shorthand for the main kinds of questions you hear:

Engagement Questions: All students offer relevant responses in orderly fashion.

Assessment Questions: One student answers at a time, often the same student(s).

Open Questions: Most students seem confused or don't know how to respond.

Teacher Answers Own: Students appear clueless; teacher supplies answers.

7. **Write ONE Recommended Action:** While you may feel tempted to list many things your teacher needs to address, be careful not to overwhelm or defeat your teacher. Instead, by identifying only one major recommendation, you create a do-able focus—a one-step-at-a-time approach to improving student engagement. For instance, if you have placed many X's in several strategy columns, you might focus your major recommendation around the strategy you think will be easiest for your teacher to fix.

Schedule Your Debriefing after Your *Time-on-Task* Observation

After your observation using a ***Time-on-Task Tool***, be sure to schedule a debriefing. The purpose of the debriefing is to guide your teacher—using the data you collected in the tool—to focus on the specific aspect of engagement you have identified.

Your initial stance with your teacher will probably be that of ***consultant*** (more about that in the next chapter.) Keep in mind that, as a consultant, you want to ask questions that will lead your teacher to make prescriptions for himself or herself. The most productive debriefing is not one in which you pronounce your recommendations or dictate next steps, but rather one in which you share data. Indeed, success in a debriefing becomes obvious when a teacher reaches a clear and productive conclusion from the data or says "Ah, ha! I think I should do. . . !"

Following is a set of debriefing steps we recommend, alongside which you will find questions, statements, and other explanations that might help you guide your teacher through the debriefing.

Guide to Debriefing after a Time-On-Task	
Steps	**Explanations (Discussion, Script)**
1 **Focus Your Discussion and Establish Rapport**	Present your major concern as one your teacher appears to feel or share. For instance, "*As I observed in your classroom today, I watched for what bothers you. It was obvious that when kids do ______, it bothers you because I see/hear you do ______. Have you been thinking about/decreasing what bothers you . . .?*"
2 **Explain the *Time-on-Task Tool***	Overview types of data you collect with a ***Time-On-Task Tool***: ♦ Intervals ♦ Percentages of actively engaged students, not just the quiet/passively engaged ♦ Anecdotal notations of observable behaviors, not opinions ♦ Examples of engaged and disengaged behaviors ♦ Engagement strategies
3 **Share the Data by Using the *Time-On-Task Tool***	If you decide not to show your teacher every line of data you collect on the tool, be sure to focus on the "Recommended Action" at the bottom. Here are possible discussion points: ♦ The "good" student engagement numbers: 80% and above, pointing out "*If a teacher can hit 80% once, he or she can do it twice, three times . . .*" ♦ Share data relating to the problem strategy (the X's and the line-by-line evidence during the intervals) ♦ Highlight in yellow the engagement strategies you want your teacher to think about
4 **Set a Goal with Your Teacher**	If student engagement in many intervals is below 50%, set an interim goal of raising it to 60% rather than the benchmark of 80%. (Refer again to the X's and reiterate the gains your teacher might make by focusing for now on this one strategy in particular.)
5 **Establish a Timeline**	Set another date with your teacher for the two of you to. . . ♦ Visit and observe for the specific strategy item your teacher is working on. (Note: Do this as quickly as possible.) ♦ Shadow your teacher for the specific item (during a subsequent visit) if your teacher is unsure about how to use the strategy. (See examples in the following strategy chapters.) ♦ Observe a demonstration teacher together.
6 **Bring Debriefing to Closure**	End on a positive note: "*I am looking forward to watching your growth in ______. I have every confidence you can do this because I saw ______.* (Again, refer to the DATA you have collected.) Always emphasize that your work together, for now, is not formal and that your role is that of a mentor rather than an administrator.

One more thing: When you conduct a debriefing, especially if you are acting as a mentor, consider meeting in the teacher's room or a conference room, but NOT in your office, which you should reserve for more formal situations. **Keeping both your tone and the location of your debriefing informal sends a powerful message of support to your teacher.**

Recognize a Successful Debriefing

The following is a transcript of the actual debriefing with 6th grade language arts teacher Samantha Samuels. Notice the six debriefing steps outlined in the preceding **Guide to Debriefing after a Time-on-Task**.

Debriefing Steps	Transcript of an Actual Debriefing
Focus	Administrator: *Hi Samantha, thanks for meeting with me. As I observed in your classroom today, I was looking for what bothers you. What I noticed was that when you would ask questions and students didn't respond, your eyes got wider, and your pacing increased. You basically looked uncomfortable.* Samantha: *YES! I felt like a dentist trying to pull teeth. This group of kids just doesn't want to respond. I don't know how they can stand being so bored.* Administrator: *It sounds like teaching will be much more fun for you if you can find ways to increase the active engagement of your students.* Samantha: *YES! Most definitely. But I do ask questions — lots of questions. They just don't answer them or they don't know the answers*
Explain Tool	Administrator: *Together, we can increase the amount of active student engagement and decrease your stress level! Let me explain the Time On Task Observation Tool that I used to collect data today. I took specific notes in 3– to 5–minute intervals. I wrote down what you were doing as it related to what the students were doing. I then placed an X by items that seem to be causing a lack of engagement and a star by the items that you were doing well.*
Use Tool to Show Data	Administrator: *Let's look at your data. You can see that you are not going to lose control of your class—you have a benchmark % of quiet (passive) students. You are very ready to move to the next step of having active students. Your Voice is working well for you, and you have established Expectations for behavior. Most students are seated and quiet.* Samantha (nodding): *Yes, a month ago, I just wanted them to sit down and be quiet! Now I want to have them participate with me, not stare at me.* Administrator: *Let's look at your data. I highlighted some items we can focus on. Interval 1 – only 1 student responded. When you asked the question,"Do we know who the main character is," how many students did you want to respond?* Samantha: *All of them! They all should know the answer.*

Debriefing Steps	Transcript of an Actual Debriefing
Use Tool to Show Data *(cont'd)*	Administrator: *So, if you were to say, "Think about who the main character is, or whisper to your neighbor who the main character is," and then call on one student to respond, you would have everyone engaged before one student responds?* (Samantha nods.) *Here are some more examples at Interval 2. You asked, "What did he say? Is that part of the conflict?" The same student responded. Could you rephrase the question so all students respond?* Samantha: *Hmmm. Since they are seated in tables, I could have them huddle and discuss the question and then call on one student to answer.* Administrator: *Yes, you would be engaging then assessing. What about the question you asked in interval 3: "Who sounds like the bad guy?"* Samantha: *I'm not sure. I don't want them to huddle every time or whisper to their neighbor. What do you think?* Administrator: *I have seen other teachers have students write the answer in the air, show with their fingers how many answers they have thought of, write the answer on a white board...Do you think any of these tactics would work with your students?* Samantha: *YES! I think all of them would. What about when I want them all to just say the answer? I assumed that all students would respond if I just asked the question, but this is not the case.* Administrator: *True. Typically teachers at your grade level teach their students a Signal. They raise their hand while asking a question when they want students to raise their hands if they know the answer and wait to be called on. If they want everyone to chorally respond, they put their hand out and say,"THINK, Who sounds like the bad guy?" The teacher then drops her hand and says, "RESPOND." This way all students have wait time and typically 80–95% will respond.* Samantha: *I could do that.*
Set a Goal	Administrator: *So, let's set a goal. In looking at the questioning tallies at the bottom of your form, you can see that you had 2 engagement tallies, 1 assessment tally, 21 open tallies, and 8 times you answered your own question. What do you think would be a realistic goal?* Samantha: *Get rid of every open question and not answer my own questions?* Administrator: *You will get there. How about we start with cutting half your open questions. . .no more than 10. Let's also set the goal to increase your engagement tallies to 10. Is this doable? I think the practice of answering your own questions will go away when you Cue students to respond.* Samantha: *YES!* Administrator: *Which engagement strategy do you want to focus on first?* Samantha: *I think I want to start with teaching my students the Signal to chorally respond.*

(continued)

Debriefing Steps	Transcript of an Actual Debriefing
Establish a Timeline	Administrator: *Sounds great. May I visit tomorrow at the same time while you are doing direct instruction and I'll only watch and collect data on your engagement, open, and assessment questions. I'll see if you are answering any of your own questions? I will script you in the appropriate column so you will know what questions you asked. After the observation, we can work together to change open questions into engagement questions.* Samantha: *OK.*
Reach Closure	Administrator: *I know that you can do this. I have watched you move from a class of students that were out of their seats, constantly talking, to students who are now seated and quiet. I know you can take this next step to move your passive students to active students. As you know, our work together on this is informal right now. I appreciate your positive attitude.* Samantha: *THANK YOU!*

Move Forward on Engagement Skills

The debriefing of grade six language arts teacher Samantha Samuels shows how engagement data led to an initial diagnosis for a teacher struggling with students' lack of responsiveness. Using the data from the *Time-on-Task Tool*, the principal's consultation with Samantha helped her set goals to decrease open and assessment questions by half, thereby increasing her focus on engagement questions.

What followed was a brief skill-observation focusing on Tasking (Chapter 10), specifically on Samantha's efforts to refocus her questions. Indeed, Samantha was quick to spot opportunities for refining her questioning—that is, for honing her use of one important engagement strategy, Tasking.

However, when teachers need more direct support and applied practice, you will find additional guided practice and tools in the skills chapters. For instance, for direct support and applied practice, you will find *Focused Observation Tools* (for quick 15–minute observations that focus specifically on one management skill,) *Depth Observation Tools* (to focus on one management skill in-depth), and *Demo Observation Tools* (to develop examples of skill mastery). Using the *Demo Observation Tool*, you would accompany your teacher to a demo teacher's classroom where both you and your teacher complete the *Demo Observation Tool*, unlocking the basic components of the demo teacher's success with the specific engagement skill.

These are the purposes, outcomes, and other essential aspects of your focused and depth data tools:

Major Skill Development Tools			
	Focused Observation Tools	**Depth Observation Tools**	**Demo Observation Tools**
Purpose	♦ Collect data and provide specific feedback about the teacher's use of a specific engagement skill.	♦ Collect additional in-depth data about the teacher's use of a specific engagement skill.	♦ Help a teacher recognize and reflect on high- performing examples of a specific engagement skill.
Outcome(s)	♦ Teacher will have specific strategies to focus on.	♦ Teacher will have a greater insight about his own use of that skill. ♦ Teacher will be able to see his own progress.	♦ Teacher will have a more complete picture of the skill. ♦ Teacher will have immediate transfer of skill specifics after actually seeing it utilized with students.
Audience	♦ New teachers. ♦ Struggling teachers.	♦ New teachers. ♦ Struggling teachers.	♦ New teachers. ♦ Struggling teachers.
Time Commitment	♦ Typically one observation per week until the skill starts to become somewhat automatic. ♦ 15–minute observation.	♦ Typically one or two observations until the skill is mastered. ♦ 20– to 30–minute observation.	♦ 20– to 30–minute observation ♦ Typically once or twice when initializing the skill.
Stance	♦ Consultant/ Evaluator.	♦ Consultant.	♦ Consultant.

Moving forward, you can use the chapters focusing on The Big Eight engagement skills to serve two general purposes: (1) to develop a good understanding of the elements of each engagement skill, and (2) to access specific steps in the consulting and coaching processes using the data collection tools available. The goal of this work is to assist you in these ways:

Recognize Each Engagement Skill in Practice. You will find one full chapter devoted to each skill.

Know How to Define and Identify an Engagement Skill. We offer clear details and concrete examples of classroom practice of each skill.

Understand Successful Uses of the Skills. Case studies present and describe diverse situations in which teachers have applied each of The Big Eight successfully and effectively.

Recognize Missed Opportunities for Using a Skill. Be alert for the kinds of situations in which teachers overlook an engagement strategy.

Understand and Use Tools for Coaching and Consulting. Explanations on the pages of these chapters also contain models of the very tools you will use. As the graphic to the right demonstrates, on-page explanations exist side by side with completed tools to show you how you might use the tool in your observations and in your consultation and coaching stances with your teachers.

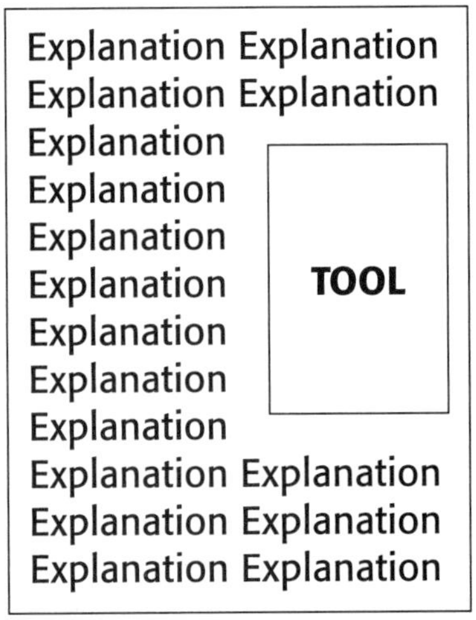

Explanation Explanation
Explanation Explanation
Explanation
Explanation
Explanation
Explanation TOOL
Explanation
Explanation
Explanation
Explanation Explanation
Explanation Explanation
Explanation Explanation

Develop Expertise in the Consulting and Coaching Processes. Each chapter outlines steps in consulting and coaching with data collection tools tailored to those stances.

Move Your Teacher toward Gradual Release. You will transition from consulting to coaching with a view toward gradually releasing your teacher. Each section provides you with engagement-specific questions you can use for your coaching conversations.

3

Moving Toward Gradual Release

Most administrators recognize that a teacher's innate talent alone does not ensure success in the classroom. Teachers begin to grow into their skills on day one—some begin to grow during their practice teaching—and much of that growth is aided and abetted by supervisors, other teachers, and by direct and indirect feedback from students. **Yes, it takes a village. . . .**

Choose Your Stance

The purpose of your supervisory actions will determine your role: evaluator or growth promoter (Glanz and Neville, 1997; Glickman, Gordon and Ross-Gordon, 2004; Glickman, 2002; Lipton, Wellman and Humbard, 2001; Joyce and Showers, 1984; Zepeda, 2007a, 2007b). Be clear in your own mind about the role you choose to perform, and communicate your role to your teachers. For instance: **You will function as an evaluator if your purpose is strictly to determine whether your teacher is meeting the standards of effective teaching (Glickman, et al., 2004).**

Normally, supervisory actions occur through formal processes in which (1) the teacher has had prior notification that an observation will occur, and (2) observation data will be used to determine performance according to standards. Since performance decisions usually have ramifications for job retention (Glickman, et al., 2004; Zepeda, 2007a), we recommend that any interactions around the formal observation take place in your office.

By contrast, if the sole purpose of your supervisory actions is to help the teacher hone skills, we recommend that interactions around these observations occur outside your office in places such as the library or the teacher's classroom in order to signal your teachers the difference between your function as an evaluator or as a promoter of teacher growth. **You will function as a mentor when your purpose is to promote teacher growth** (Glickman, et al., 2004; Lipton, et al., 2001).

The ultimate goal in your work with teachers is gradual release. The conscious roles or stances you take will facilitate the process of getting there.

Here are five stances you will most likely take in working with your teachers, a significant portion of which will be observing, consulting, and coaching (Glickman, et al., 2004; Lipton, et al., 2001.) In effect, the following are your courses of action in providing assistance:

Administrator's Action Stances

Stance	Definition	When to Use the Stance
Evaluator	To dictate	♦ Teacher is not willing to see his/her own problems. ♦ Problematic situation where termination is a possible result. ♦ Teacher does not own his/her problems in the classroom.
Consultant	To tell and show	♦ Teacher does not have the knowledge. ♦ Teacher cannot see his/her own problems. ♦ Teacher shows lack of assessment of students or self.
Bridge Consultant or Coach	To ask and tell	♦ Teacher wants to make a change or try a new strategy, but is unsure or not willing to chance mistakes. ♦ Teacher is unaware of what is causing certain situations, but through looking at data is able to take ownership of the situation and make necessary changes.
Coach	To ask	♦ Teacher desires to focus on a certain objective and to assess if objective has been met. ♦ Teacher is an innovator and desires to try new teaching strategies. ♦ Teacher is concerned about meeting the various needs of students.
Collaborator	To share	♦ Teacher and administrator both have knowledge (of a problem) and in combination can create new outcomes.

Many times it is difficult to determine when to move from one stance to the next. Consider these parameters: **If you choose only to consult, then you are making an assumption that you have expertise that your teacher does not**, thus assuming 80% of the responsibility for identifying the areas to improve and for selecting strategies your teacher can use to improve. **If you move to a coaching stance, then you are making an assumption that your teacher has high levels of expertise and can identify areas for refinement, can set goals, and can develop a time-bound action plan for achieving these goals.** In the coaching stance, then, your are assuming 20% of the responsibility with your teacher taking a much larger role to implement an improvement plan with students (Glickman, et al., 2004).

Move toward Gradual Release

Remember that your process with most teachers will begin with consulting. Don't lose sight of this important element in helping your teacher climb aboard your process comfortably and with buy-in. At the same time, avoid working too long in your own comfort zone rather than differentiating, or switching, stances as needed to meet your teacher's individual needs (Glickman, et al., 2004; Lipton, et al., 2001).

Think of gradual release as sending your wonderful creature back into the wild to grow [further] and to thrive. This is your goal in working with your treacher. To reach the gradual release stage, you will need to take a coaching stance, but if you move to this stance too quickly your teacher may feel frustrated or, worse, may slip back into familiar and comfortable routines of problematic teaching. It may be your new teachers who are most likely not to respond readily to a coaching relationship because they may not yet have the knowledge and experience to correct their own behavior (Glickman, et al., 2004; Glickman, 2002; Lipton, et al., 2001; Wellman & Lipton, 2004). Wait until your teacher is ready for your coaching stance to allow him or her to move at a pace that feels natural.

Process Model for Achieving Gradual Release

Phase toward Gradual Release	Before Your Observation	During Your Observation	After Your Observation
Diagnosis		Observe	Consult
Level One	Consult	Observe	Consult
Level Two Bridge	Coach	Observe	Consult
Level Three	Coach	Observe	Coach

Diagnosis Phase

In the first phase of your process, especially with a new or struggling teacher, you will use a *Time-on-Task Tool* to observe for your teacher's major strengths and weaknesses. This is your initial diagnosis and does not require a conversation prior to the observation. Your consultation with your teacher will follow your observation, at which time you will use your data from the *Time-on-Task Tool* to show your teacher the strong points as well as one area for refinement. You may return to this phase (see Gradual Release Model above) several times in order to diagnose or identify the areas in which your teacher has made progress and the areas needing focus next. **Schematically, your diagnosis phase looks like this:**

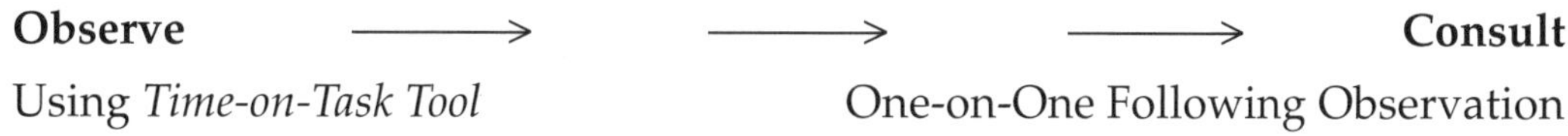

Level One: Consultation Phase

The next step toward Gradual Release is to work with your teacher on one specific area of focus, a phase in which you will use *Focused Observation Tools*. It is very helpful to consult (tell and show) with your teacher before the observation explicitly telling and showing the one skill that you will be focusing on during your 15–minute observation.

Consult	⟶	**Observe**	⟶	**Consult**
One-on-One Prior to Observation		Using *Focused Observation Tool*		One-on-One Following Observation

After the observations, have a consultation to show and describe your teacher's growth and determine together ONE area for refinement. This step may occur more than once. Typically, this step takes about two to three weeks with a Focused Observation every week, and it also is an excellent time during the gradual release process to take your teacher to observe a demonstration teacher (using *Demo Observation Tools*) so your teacher can see exactly what the specific skill looks like and sounds like.

Level Two: Bridge Phase

This next step represents a major change in focus. Your role moves from that of telling a teacher what to do and how to do it to that of coach in which you show trust in your teacher to make the right instructional decisions with opportunities to reflect on performance. Once your teacher demonstrates some knowledge of the engagement skill(s) in focus, you can move fully into a coaching stance. For instance, you can become your teacher's coach prior to the next lesson you will observe, helping him or her practice or think through the lesson several times before actually conducting it. You may find that *Depth Observation Tools* are very helpful during this phase.

Coach	⟶	**Observe**	⟶	**Consult**
One-on-One Prior to Observation		Using *Focused Observation Tool*		One-on-One Following Observation

During this Bridge Phase, you should keep in mind that your teacher may falter, particularly if he or she does not yet have the full knowledge necessary to unlock his or her own growth. In these instances, you may need to return to consultation routines (telling and showing) after an observation.

Level Three: Full Coaching Phase

As your teacher begins to show more competence and takes more ownership of the challenges involved in a certain engagement skill, you will know that it is time to move into a full coaching relationship. Your teacher now becomes responsible for 80% of the decisions. Again, you can utilize *Depth Observation Tools* for this coaching cycle, or you can tailor the tools to collect certain kinds of data your teacher needs or desires. It is always a good thing when your teacher shows interest and curiosity about the fine points in executing an engagement skill.

Coach	⟶	**Observe**	⟶	**Coach**
One-on-One Prior to Observation		Using a Tool Created to Address Teacher Question(S)		One-On-One Following Observation

This final step toward full release involves coaching (asking) before the lesson to assist your teacher with thinking through the lesson, its potential problems and desired outcomes, while providing a sounding board after the lesson for the teacher to reflect and to self-direct his or her learning for the future. Teachers—good teachers, for sure—need to be coached so they can have opportunities to examine their strengths and refinements in their own world of classroom performance. As Stephen Barkley (2005) told an audience at the National Staff Development Conference (NSDC), "The most skilled and professional educators should be coached the most."

Tailor Your Data Collection To Meet Specialized Teacher Needs

Many times, teachers request data for which the coach must use or create special tools. The next chart lists frequently-asked questions teachers pose about their own teaching and identifies the tools that will help collect the requisite data. The tools described in the following chart can be found in the Appendix (pp. 156–161):

Additional Tools for Coaching and Answering Your Teacher's Questions

Teacher Question	Tool	Purpose
Are my directions understandable?	***Teacher Action/ Student Response Tool***	To record teacher actions and student responses and percentage of engagement during intervals of instruction.
Am I differentiating instruction to meet individual needs?	***Differentiation Observation Tool***	To collect teacher actions and student responses in relation to academic levels of learners.
Are my questions promoting active engagement?	***Questioning Observation Tool***	To guide or script teacher's types of questions.
Am I using cooperative learning effectively?	***Cooperative Learning Observation Tool***	To track areas of student behaviors vital for cooperative learning.

(continued)

Additional Tools for Coaching and Answering Your Teacher's Questions		
How do I know students are ready to go from direct instruction to guided practice to independent practice?	***Lesson Sequence Observation Tool***	To track a lesson through instructional components while assessing student engagement.
How do I handle student(s) with difficult behaviors?	***Engagement vs. Individual Students(s) Tool***	To compare rates of on-task behavior of all students versus the engagement levels of one or two students.

Emphasize Engagement Strategies

Engagement means active involvement of students in their own learning. Research strongly suggests that students' academic success depends in large part on their engagement in instruction (Greenwood, Terry, Marquis, and Walker, 1994).

Engagement skills are the behaviors teachers employ to facilitate academic success. These behaviors are specific *strategy actions* that teachers learn—in part, through their instincts and good common sense, but more so through heightened awareness of the needs of children and through practice encouraged and sharpened by others such as you and others who collaborate.

The net result of the sound practice of a teacher's engagement skills is its effect on students, who consciously and unconsciously respond in ways you can observe and measure.

Helping teachers focus on their engagement skills may involve several important steps:

- Identify and define engagement skills generally and specifically,
- Communicate on a regular basis the importance of engagement skills on teacher success and student achievement,
- Promote dialogue with and among teachers about the specific engagement skills they possess as well as those they can sharpen, and
- Develop strategies for teachers—with their participation, over time, and as necessary—to improve their performance and to increase student learning.

The goal of administrative supervision is to increase student learning—first by hiring and retaining effective teachers and second by creating an environment in which teachers continually refine their skills (Glickman, 2002; Glickman, 2004). This goal is never more important than in meeting the needs of teachers who struggle to meet standards of effective teaching practices (Zepeda, 2007a, 2007b). The purpose of this book is to provide for principals—and all who work collaboratively with teachers—the knowledge and skills that can be used to help all teachers grow with special emphasis on assisting teachers who struggle. **Using the tools of consulting and coaching may be your most efficient and effective means of helping your teachers master engagement skills and producing the greatest instructional growth in the shortest amount of time.**

To share and explain the observation-evaluation-assistance process you plan to use during the school year, you might convey your goals with general statements like the ones that follow:

Orient Staff to Your Process	
Your Goals	**Sample Statements**
A Clarify purpose(s) of observations and evaluations according to national and/or district standards (Chapter 1)	A *My formal evaluations are based on district standards that can serve as a guide for you to self-assess and set individual growth goals.*
B Define roles, as applicable: principal, assistant principal, coach, mentor, consultant (Chapter 2)	B *As administrator, I serve in many roles:* *As* principal, *I am an evaluator (among other responsibilities).* *As* mentor, *I serve you as a consultant, your informal helper with student engagement, and as a coach, your informal facilitator of in-depth conversations about your teaching.*
C Identify and define district "domains" for teacher evaluation (Chapters 1 and 12)	C *Our district identifies four domains for teacher evaluation:* *Domain I: Instruction and Assessment* *Domain II: Planning and Preparation* *Domain III: Learning Environment* *Domain IV: Professionalism*
D Define and describe the Engagement Skills you will evaluate (Chapters 4 to 11)	D *Our school goal is to increase active student engagement. The engagement skills we will focus on this year are Expectations, Attention Prompts, Proximity, Cueing, Signals, Time Limits, Tasking, and Voice.*
E Describe relationship-building aspects of your process	E *My goal is to help you increase the engagement levels of your students. In a mentoring stance (consulting or coaching), we will meet in your classroom or a conference room. When we are debriefing or planning for a formal observation, I will act as an evaluator, and we will meet in my office.*

Chapter 4

Expectations

Skill #1

The Big Eight Engagement Skills

Expectations Teacher ensures that students know what to do and when and how to do it.
ATTENTION PROMPTS
PROXIMITY
CUEING
SIGNALS
TIME LIMITS
TASKING
VOICE

4

Expectations
Skill #1

TOOLS for Evaluating EXPECTATIONS

See Appendix pp. 162–164

CASE STUDY

Thelma Porter had a difficult year which she felt owed in part to a difficult group of 2nd graders. By fall of her second year, Thelma felt desperate. Her students were off task and unruly, particularly during independent work times, which made small group instruction nearly impossible. She felt frustrated and irritable.

After explaining the consulting and coaching process to Thelma, the principal made an appointment to take baseline data using the *Time-on-Task Tool* (See Thelma's on p. 40.) Her student engagement levels sat mostly between 6% and 25% briefly spiking to between 34% and 50%. Students did not know what *being on task* looked and sounded like. Furthermore, Thelma was not reinforcing those few students who *were* on task. Together, Thelma and her principal articulated what *being on task* should look and sound like and then devised a plan to teach those Expectations to her students using four steps:

1. Explain the behavior,
2. Demonstrate the behavior,
3. Give guided practice, and
4. Refine the behavior through reinforcement and reteaching.

Most students want a clear understanding of what they are expected to do. As you visit classrooms with high levels of student engagement, you probably will notice that teachers remind students of, or set **Expectations** for, ways in which they should function or behave. **In classrooms where teachers have clarified and maintained Expectations, student engagement and learning appear high, and transitions flow effortlessly from one activity to another** (Colvin, et al, 1997; DePry & Sugai, 2002; Johnson, et al, 1996; Lane, et al, 2003.) These teachers make running a classroom look so effortless that an uninformed observer may think this teacher just lucked out with a good group of students. What might not be readily apparent, however, is how the teacher has set, communicated, refined, and reinforced Expectations that optimize student learning. You'll know when Expectations have been set—and are operating well—and you will recognize when Expectations are lacking.

***Expectations* are specific behaviors and procedures effective teachers identify for students to follow, creating an environment that supports optimal student learning.** Let's look at Expectations in two categories: *immediate Expectations* and *habitual Expectations*. ***Immediate Expectations* are student behaviors and procedures that occur in real time, differing from one lesson or circumstance to the next.** For example, a lesson might require students to write answers in columns on a form, and the teacher's immediate Expectation is that students will follow the direction to do so. In another instance, a teacher might communicate the immediate Expectation that students will assemble popsicle sticks to illustrate a math principle. Immediate Expectations are the behavioral part of instruction. Skilled teachers identify immediate Expectations ahead of time for each lesson and then communicate them clearly before students are given permission to start the learning activity. Students will meet immediate Expectations much better if a few critical habitual Expectations have been established.

***Habitual Expectations* are behaviors and procedures that are long term and present in nearly every lesson and circumstance of classroom life.** For example, students will always focus when their teacher gives an Attention Prompt (Chapter 5). Here's another: Students will always start themselves on work when they enter the classroom; they are expected to move silently with intent when walking around the classroom. These procedural habits are at the heart of a high-functioning classroom. Wise teachers invest time and effort at the beginning of the year to teach habitual Expectations in ways that ensure students grasp two important things: first, a clear understanding of what the habit looks like and sounds like, and second, that in this teacher's classroom all students are required to meet that Expectation (Gudmundsen, Williams, & Lybert, 1996.) By teachers investing time and effort to teach the habit and then maintain it by using Proximity (Chapter 6) and Cueing (Chapter 7), these habitual Expectations provide the underpinnings of a high-functioning classroom.

Habitual behaviors become routine because students follow them automatically. Habits are internalized.

Successful teachers frequently follow a set of simple steps with their students to establish long-term Expectations for certain procedures or behaviors. Your teachers may find success with a

CASE STUDY – *cont'd*

With her principal shadowing from the back of her room, Thelma began the process right before moving into independent work time so she could reinforce students on task and redirect as needed. She re-taught *on-task* behavioral Expectations to three students during recess and to two others during the next recess.

The next visit, her principal took data using another *Time-on-Task Tool* and found her levels of engagement averaging between 34% and 50% with spikes between 51% and 79%. The data suggested Thelma was recognizing her on-task students but was limiting her reinforcing comments to *"good job"* and *"thank you."*

Since Thelma also needed work on Cueing, her principal taught her how to incorporate more specific Cues (see Chapter 7) to recognize good behavior and to reinforce Expectations. Together they used the *Looks Like/Sounds Like* chart Thelma had developed earlier with students to develop these Cues:

Thank you, Sean, for getting to work so quickly. I noticed Billy has worked for 5 minutes without pause.

A few days later, the principal used coaching questions to help Thelma reflect on patterns she saw in the data. For one thing, she noticed high engagement during the first 10 minutes of work time with gradual loss of focus during the last 5. For another, all Cues but one occurred during the first 7 minutes. Thelma set a goal to spread Cues throughout work periods and to refine phrasing. Eventually, with more coaching she mastered all engagement skills, including Expectations, and now coaches other struggling teachers in her district.

sequence of four steps, which you will find presented in greater detail later in this chapter (Gudmundsen, et al., 1996.) Here they are in brief:

- **Describe** the Expectation (procedure or behavior).
  Consider using a descriptive graphic like a *Looks Like/Sounds Like* chart.
- **Demonstrate** the Expectation: e.g., role-playing.
- **Practice** the Expectation: e.g., trial runs.
- **Refine** as needed: e.g., reteach and self-reflect.

As part of the first step, develop a *Looks Like/Sounds Like* chart that will help students visualize an Expectation. This is the chart used by Thelma Porter in this chapter's Case Study:

Being on Task	
Looks Like – Sit at desk – Work quietly – Avoid talking – Don't bother other students – Do choice activities when assignment done	**Sounds Like** – Quiet – Soft whisper of pencils moving on paper

Elements of Expectations

We urge you to recognize the hallmarks of Expectations in your classroom observations and to help teachers develop or hone this fundamental, critical skill.

Recognize Immediate Expectations. Your teacher will regularly encounter classroom situations calling for unique ways that students must conduct themselves. If your teacher has set Expectations effectively, students in that class will act in ways that allow learning to occur. Typically, such behaviors will include (1) what students should do when their assigned work is completed, (2) how they must behave, such as quietly standing up, sitting down, or moving hands during a particular part of a lesson, (3) when students will follow a one-time procedure such as going to the gym to have their eyes checked. When teachers identify immediate Expectations and communicate them to students before the learning activity begins, they save time and optimize learning.

Recognize Habitual Expectations. These are the particular routines or ways in which work gets done. Some procedures are quite simple while others may be more complex and require the building of habits. Simple procedures include customary processes for passing out and collecting papers, lining up to move from Point A to Point B, giving teachers Attention when prompted—even a procedure for going to the gym for Physical Education, when properly executed, is a procedural Expectation. Other procedures have already been learned—homework or project Expectations, for instance—so these may be observable in student output such as sharing answers or readiness for the next step in a process or the simple turning-in of work product.

Here are the components of one teacher's habitual Expectations for going to the gym. Upon receiving the teacher's prompt, students follow this routine:

- Students line up in relative silence and show respect for each other's personal space.
- They move silently to the gym upon seeing their teacher nod.
- Students sit on the gym steps talking quietly, anticipating class to start.
- When prompted, all students stop talking to listen for directions.

An observer of this process would understand that Expectations have been set by the teacher and are fully understood by students.

In another example of habitual Expectations, it becomes clear to an observer that students have learned what is expected following homework assignments. As these students arrive in class, they do the following:

- Students take their seats and remove their composition binders.
- They remove written drafts of essays and place them on their desks by the time the bell rings.
- When prompted, all students appear ready to discuss their drafts.

You will observe more complex procedures, of course, which may include self-starting activities, students' uses of learning centers, the handling of equipment and supplies such as math manipulatives, and academic procedures such as partner reading, proper conduct of science experiments, or cooperative learning.

Here is another example of habitual Expectations: Mrs. Lawrence, a fifth grade teacher, planned for her school year to include students frequently working in learning centers while others receive small group instruction. Mrs. Lawrence understood that this would require students functioning independently, so in setting Expectations, she began her year by developing independence, teaching her students to self-start whenever they entered her classroom and after any recess or other break. Only after her students got into the routine of self-starting did Mrs. Lawrence find transferring that behavior to learning centers relatively easy. Now, as reinforcement for Expectations, this teacher reminds students that when they complete the work for one learning center, they put their materials away and move quietly to the next. Movement from one learning center to the next is a series of self-starts that are linked together.

Be aware that complex procedures may require significant time and effort for your teacher to establish. When you see students performing complex procedures with little confusion and without off-task behavior, you will know that your teacher has done a good job of setting Expectations. When you see students fail to perform complex procedures competently or cooperatively, you will know that your teacher needs to catch up, which may require some time and effort.

As you observe, keep in mind the two main categories—immediate and habitual Expectations—as you judge the effectiveness of your teacher's approaches to setting Expectations. Recognizing these categories will help you identify strengths and weaknesses and may help you focus direction for helping a teacher in need.

Effective and Ineffective Expectations

Kind of Expectation	Ineffective Expectation	Effective Expectation
Immediate Expectations (Short Term)	Teacher allows students to choose one of three books to read for literacy circles but does not give clear Expectations. Teacher spends an extra 10 minutes attempting to clarify with comments such as *Everybody, I told you to get your books and start reading. Okay, students, quiet down. Don't forget to write your name by the book title! All right! Everybody back in your seats . . . NOW!*	Teacher allows students to choose one of three books to read for literacy circles and gives the following clear Expectations about the activity: *When I call your name, I expect you to do three things:* 1. *Select one of the three literature books,* 2. *Write your name on the board under its title, and* 3. *Return quietly to your seat to begin reading your book*
Habitual Expectation (Long Term)	Because the teacher had not taught students Expectations (procedures) for entering the room at the beginning of the day and after recess breaks, teacher spends extra time reminding students to get to work. *Let's get to work now! Okay, students, start on your assignment. Students, quiet down now; it's time to get to work.*	At the beginning of the year, the teacher uses the four-step process to teach students the habit of starting themselves on work at the beginning of the day and after recess. Teacher spends time reinforcing students for self-starting. *Table 3, thank you for getting right on task. Joe, you got your materials out immediately.*

Because Expectations may vary from teacher to teacher, no single set of Expectations—that is, no short list of tactics for ***setting*** Expectations—will work with every teacher at every level, nor will every teacher follow the same roadmap in setting those Expectations. However, you should keep this in mind: **Effective teachers develop Expectations by knowing *in advance* the immediate or habitual outcomes they desire of their students**. To get there, the teacher makes a careful analysis of his or her instructional practices as well as specific learning experiences to create for students. For each major area of instruction, these teachers ask themselves, *What behaviors or procedures do my students need to understand (or develop) so they can succeed in this type of learning?* The successful teacher maps out those behaviors by setting Expectations early, clearly, and consistently.

Understand Setting Expectations Is a Process. It starts at the beginning of the school year. An effective teacher communicates major Expectations at the outset, expecting to refine and reinforce these Expectations regularly and consistently. Some teachers begin setting Expectations with their very first words of the year—Expectations about classroom procedures, ways in which individuals and groups will function on tasks, homework habits, behavioral Expectations, and so on. Some teachers post certain Expectations in conspicuous places in their classrooms, some write Expectations on handouts for students, others weave certain Expectations into their daily classroom communication—the possibilities for conveying Expectations may be endless, but they are essential, critical, mandatory.

When you first recognize that your teacher is having difficulty with Expectations, you probably will recognize one or more of the eight skills that your teacher needs to address in addition to this one. Use your judgment in deciding on which order—and how many skills at a time—to address with your teacher. It makes sense to address Expectations early in the year because behaviors and procedures don't fall into place over night, and you may need to link another skill into your discussions of Expectations. In this chapter's case study, Thelma Porter's principal focused on Cueing as well as Expectations, and the teacher discovered that working on one reinforced her work on the other.

You can see the *Time-On-Task Tool* that Thelma's principal completed on the next page.

Recognizing Successful Uses of Expectations

Teachers who succeed at setting Expectations have thought through their instructional goals and strategies. To be sure, they have identified key behaviors and procedures they believe will help students perform at high levels in their classrooms. And once they have identified their Expectations, these teachers share them in a variety of ways with their students and then refine them over time through use of positive Cueing, Proximity, and whatever other strategies help bring students up to standards.

Following are examples of three teachers who increased productive learning significantly by identifying, communicating, and refining Expectations.

Example 1: 3rd Grade Reading Class

Mrs. Sharp has become a master at establishing and communicating immediate Expectations. For example, things went very smoothly on the day she gave her students a reading assignment that she knew would be complicated. She told students to identify the four main parts of a story they had read independently, and she listed these on the board: main character(s), setting, main problem or conflict, and plot events that led to the main problem. To communicate her Expectations, she devised a quick system for her students to follow:

1. *"Fold your paper into four squares."* (Mrs. Sharp demonstrates with a model piece of paper as she verbalizes the instructions);
2. *"Label each square with one of the four parts of a story."* (She writes on her model);
3. *"Fill in each square with the other parts of the story: characters, setting, problem."*

Time-On-Task (Observation Tool for All Engagement Skills)

Name: *Thelma Porter* Date: *Nov. 16, 2009* # Students: *18* Grade/Class: *2nd Grade* Observer: *Ms. Caroli*

Directions: Record the time for each observation you make of educator involvement in learning. Record observations as follows:

1. Mark percentage of student engagement. (P) passive, (A) active
2. Describe teacher actions causing disengagement.
3. Describe relevant student behavior, especially off-task behavior.
4. Ask yourself, "What would I do if I were the teacher?"
5. Check recommended action(s)—those things that you would do if you were the teacher. You may also want to ★ actions that the teacher performs well.

FOR EACH INTERVAL, show % of Student Engagement.

WRITE **A** for alert, attentive behavior, or **P** for passive, disengaged behavior. **THEN DESCRIBE**

INTERVALS	% Engaged	Teacher Actions Impacting Students (Below)	Student Engagement and Behavior (Below)	Expectations	Attention Prompts	Proximity	Cueing	Signals	Time Limits	Tasking	Voice
Interval No. 1 10:00 am Transition to seat	___ 0–5% ___ 6–25% *A* 26–33% ___ 34–50% *P* 51–79% ___ 80–100%	**Teacher Actions:** *After teaching the math lesson, t. gave students instructions for their independent seat work—sat at desk.*	**Student Behavior:** *3 on task immediately, 5 more after one minute, 4 more after three minutes, 6 not on task.*	X	X	X	X				
Interval No. 2 10:05 am Independent work	___ 0–5% *A* 6–25% ___ 26–33% ___ 34–50% *P* 51–79% ___ 80–100%	**Teacher Actions:** *1. Looked up! Shhh...Shhh! Shhhh! 2. Tried to redirect individual S., yelled at Sam and Troy to get on task!*	**Student Behavior:** *Noise increasing. gradually all but 3 off-task—5 shuffling in desks, 4 wondering, Sam and Troy tussling 2. Only 2 got back on task*	X		X	X				X
Interval No. 3 10:10 am Independent work	___ 0–5% *A* 6–25% ___ 26–33% ___ 34–50% *P* 51–79% ___ 80–100%	**Teacher Actions:** *Told everyone to get to seats and get on task (3 shrugged when I asked what on task looked and sounded like). Took Sam and Troy back to seat: frustration–voice & body language 2. Resumed grading papers-noise increased.*	**Student Behavior:** *1. Sam and Troy back to seat, but not on task. Rest at seats & quiet. 8 on task 2. After 2 minutes all but 3 students deteriorated into off task noisy behavior.*	X			X				X
Interval No. 4 10:15 am Independent work	___ 0–5% *A* 6–25% ___ 26–33% *P* 34–50% ___ 51–79% ___ 80–100%	**Teacher Actions:** *1. Stands.Angrily threatens that if S. don't stay at seats & on task, no am recess for anyone. 2. sits @ desk, grade papers. . .*	**Student Behavior:** *14 of 18 at seat & quiet, 11 on task stayed quiet or on task until t. sat down and began working . Almost on signal all but 4 S, began horsing around, talking loudly, pencil fights. . .*	X		X	X				X
Interval No. 5 10:20 am Independent work	___ 0–5% *A* 6–25% ___ 26–33% ___ 34–50% *P* 51–79% ___ 80–100%	**Teacher Actions:** *1. Keeps working, ignores chaos 2. Exploded, "get to seat, put heads on desk and be quiet. How expect to learn anything when can't be on task for even 2 min!"*	**Student Behavior:** *1. 3 on task 2. All but 2 heads down, 2 others mimicked t. to each other.*	X		X	X				X

Recommended Actions: *Two major issues to begin with, then tackle others, including proximity, voice, etc.*

- *Clarify and communicate student Expectations during times when students are working independently.*
- *Use social Cues to maintain behavior.*

Reproducible: Page 155, Appendix

Her principal rated Mrs. Sharp's use of Expectations with a check-plus and noted that the care she took to identify Expectations and communicate them contributed to the high levels of student engagement in her classroom. He attributed students' high-quality work on that assignment to his teacher's use of visual and kinesthetic modalities in conveying her immediate Expectations.

Example 2: 6th Grade Self-Starting

Mr. Santillo is noted for having 95% of his students engaged in work within one minute of entering his classroom. When a colleague asked for the secret of his success, he cited his investments of time and effort on the first days of school to teach the habit of self-starting, which he described as a habitual Expectation—each day, when students enter the classroom, they are to start work immediately.

Here's how Mr. Santillo did it: Prior to teaching the habit, he brought his students to a meeting place away from their desks where he devoted 15 to 20 minutes to teaching the self-starting procedure using the following four-step method:

Step 1: Describe the Habit. He **described** the importance of self-starting, focusing in particular on how it would help students learn at high levels in his classroom. Then he led students through the development of a chart that detailed what self-starting looks like and sounds like. The chart helped crystallize the self-starting procedure.

Self-Starting (SS)	
Looks Like	**Sounds Like**
– Put stuff away – Go right to seat – Look at directions – Get SS materials out – Begin SS work immediately – Work quietly	– Quiet voices when enter room – Silence of students not talking – Soft whisper of pencils writing or pages turning

Step 2: Demonstrate the Habit. He **demonstrated** self-starting by having two students whom he had selected and coached prior to the class meeting demonstrate the wrong way and then the right way. After each role play, Mr. Santillo used a *Looks Like/Sounds Like* chart to lead the class in a discussion of what the role players did correctly and what they could improve about their self-starting.

Step 3: Practice the Habit. The teacher gave students guided **practice** on self-starting with a trial run; students practiced coming in from recess and self-starting a math quiz. Mr. Santillo reminded students that they were practicing the right way to self-start.

Step 4: Refine the Habit. Over time, Mr. Santillo **refined** the Expectation of self-starting in two ways. First, he used Cueing (Chapter 7) to recognize students who were self-starting appropriately and to redirect students who were not. The *Looks Like/Sounds Like* chart for self-starting served as his source for developing specific Cueing statements. Second, he identified students who did not exhibit self-starting Expectations and retaught the procedure to them during recess breaks.

Example 3: 5th Grade Hands-on Science

If you were to observe Mrs. Ramirez's 5th grade science lessons, particularly her success with using the scientific method to conduct experiments, you would agree with her principal's observation that 95% of students appear engaged in productive learning. You might even spot Mrs. Ramirez effortlessly redirecting the occasional off-task student.

Mrs. Ramirez would be the first to tell you that her high engagement levels result from the steps she took during the first weeks of school. Specifically, she taught students the procedures for participating in this type of learning first by analyzing and planning for the key behaviors in the processes her students would need to follow. She identified teachable chunks—that is, specific steps she could introduce and practice with her students one day at a time. This process took Mrs. Ramirez about four or five days using a four-step procedure similar to the one used by Mr. Santillo, only one that required more time—**Describe. Show. Practice. Refine**—as follows:

- **Day one: Describe** (and show) the science supplies and equipment that experiments will require students to use.
- **Day two: Show** (and demonstrate) how to handle and use the equipment paying particular attention to fragile pieces like beakers and potentially dangerous pieces like Bunsen burners. Consider asking volunteers to summarize.
- **Day three: Practice** specific steps like finding and replacing pieces of equipment in their right locations. Consider asking students to role-play in demonstrating proper uses of equipment.
- **Days four and five: Refine,** as necessary, by performing trial runs and by guiding students' uses of equipment—and the scientific method—to conduct the first of the semester's experiments. Consider guiding debriefings with a focus on analyzing procedures.

During the second week, Mrs. Ramirez's students participated in two very simple science experiments with a focus on practicing the process they learned the week before. In addition to reminding students of the procedures, Mrs. Ramirez used positive Cueing to draw attention to the tasks that individuals and groups of students were doing well and to clarify Expectations. Here are a few examples of Cues she used: *Roger, I noticed that you handled the glass beakers carefully with both hands; Noel, thank you for reading all the directions before starting your experiment;* and *Sam, your group performed your tasks exactly in the way laid out in the directions.* After each pilot experiment, students self-assessed their ability to follow the procedures. As necessary, Mrs. Ramirez made appointments to reteach the proper science procedures during free time to students who were not yet following Expectations.

Note about Looks Like/Sounds Like Charts: Rarely is it a bad idea for your teacher to present a visual demonstration as part of describing an Expectation, and surely the device can only benefit visual and auditory learners. For instance, your teacher might reinforce a *Looks Like/Sounds Like* chart by placing its items into a checklist. Here's another from Example 3: Mrs.Ramirez might have added a picture of a proper science station to reinforce her Expectation.

Recognizing Missed Opportunities for Expectations

Be alert for classroom situations in which your teacher could have used Expectations but failed to do so. Following are a sample of commonly missed opportunities in which students in the classroom would most likely have functioned more productively.

Immediate Expectations (Short Term)		
Classroom Situations	**Expectation Failure**	**Solution**
1. When students turn in forms that are to go to the office, they pile forms sloppily. Some are missing.	Teacher does not give students a specific place or precise way in which the forms were to be positioned.	Give students precise Expectations for turning in the forms. *Students, when I call your table, these are my Expectations:* ♦ *Put your form in the box I placed on the desk by the door.* ♦ *Place your form facing up with the top of it by the orange arrow.*
2. As students complete their assigned work, the classroom becomes increasingly chaotic despite teacher's alternate activity written on the board.	Teacher does not communicate clearly her Expectation for what students should do when they finish an activity.	As part of giving directions for assigned tasks, teacher gives Expectations for what students may do when finished. She writes them on the board and says, *Once you complete the assignment, I expect you to do one of these three things* (points to list)*:* ♦ *Work on brain teasers individually.* ♦ *Work with a partner on word puzzles.* ♦ *Draw.* In your mind, picture which of these activities you would like to do.

<table>
<tr><th colspan="3">Habitual Expectations (Long Term)</th></tr>
<tr><th>Classroom Situations</th><th>Expectation Failure</th><th>Solution</th></tr>
<tr><td>1. Teacher spends 5 to 10 minutes settling students down after every recess break.</td><td>Teacher fails to teach students to start themselves on work immediately when they enter the room.</td><td>Develop Looks Like/Sounds Like chart to explain self-starting. Reinforce with positive Cueing, e.g., "I notice 15 students have already read directions and have started their work. . ."
<table>
<tr><th colspan="2">Self-Starting (SS)</th></tr>
<tr><td>Looks Like
– Enter classroom in an orderly way
– Put coats, etc. away
– Go directly to seat
– Read SS directions
– Get materials out
– Start work on assignment within one minute</td><td>Sounds Like
– Quiet
– Pencils moving softly on paper</td></tr>
</table></td></tr>
<tr><td>2. Students yell out and talk over each other making a math lesson chaotic and nonproductive.</td><td>Teacher fails to teach students the behavioral Expectations for giving their attention to the teacher.</td><td>Use the four-step process to teach students to raise their hands and wait before commenting or asking a question. Explain reason for raising hands. Develop Looks Like/Sounds Like chart. Use guided practice in simulated discussion. Refine by reteaching as necessary.</td></tr>
<tr><td>3. Teacher spends 20 minutes at the end of each day to reorganize learning centers that students leave messy.</td><td>Teacher fails to set and teach students standards for cleanup and for putting away materials in centers.</td><td>Use four-step method to introduce each learning center. Describe procedures for the center. Develop Looks Like/Sounds Like chart detailing proper way to get out, use, and put away materials. Demonstrate procedures to students, highlighting important points. Guide students through a practice session. Refine and reteach for students who don't get it. Use positive Cueing for students who follow proper procedures.</td></tr>
</table>

Practically everything your teacher oversees in the classroom involves setting Expectations of one kind or another. You will probably not be able to observe, evaluate, or consult about all of these, but you probably *will* choose one or two areas of Expectations. If you think your teacher has significant work to do in setting Expectations, you might focus on ones (1) you consider most critical to student learning, and (2) you think your teacher can improve most readily.

Following are some key areas in which all teachers need to establish Expectations purposefully with their students. In your observations, particularly early in the school year, look specifically for the following behaviors and procedures:

Key Areas for Observing Expectations

- Procedures for the beginning and ending of the school day.
- Transitions such as leaving and returning to the classroom, use of the bathroom, use of the cafeteria, fire and disaster drills.
- Uses of materials and equipment, including distributing and collecting materials; storage of common materials; use of drinking fountain, sink, pencil sharpener, etc.
- Group Work, including movement in and out of group, and behaviors expected of students in the group as well as those not in the group.
- Seatwork and Teacher-Led Activities, including student attention during presentations, participation, talking among students, obtaining help, out-of-seat behavior, behavior when work is completed.

Consulting for Expectations

When you consult with your teacher about Expectations, you may need to clarify the kinds of behaviors that you will observe and evaluate. Review the difference between immediate and habitual Expectations, and discuss specific ones that contribute to a positive and productive learning environment. Be sure to ask your teacher to describe some behaviors and procedures that he or she planned for and developed as habits in the classroom.

For your consultations with teachers regarding Expectations, you will find tools for observing and evaluating this skill. The *Focused Observation Tool* on the next page is one you would use when observing with a focus on Expectations probably at a time *after* you had observed with a *Time-on-Task Tool* and decided to look more closely at your teacher's use of Expectations. In this example, the principal's observation notes show

Expectations Focused Observation Tool

Name: *Mr. Blair* Date: *3/18/09*
Grade/Subject: *4th* Observer: *J.Heinz*

Directions: Observe student behaviors and procedures as they reflect teacher's Expectations.

✓ = Competent example of Expectations
✓+ = Excellent example of Expectations
✓– = Ineffective attempt of Expectations

The teacher . . .

✓	communicates immediate Expectations clearly
✓+	communicates clear Expectations for simple procedures such as giving and getting Attention, entering the classroom, self-starting, moving within classroom, etc.
–	communicates clear Expectations for complex procedures such as participating in learning centers, using math manipulatives, partner reading, cooperative learning

Observation Notes:

Keepers:

You told students that you would know they were ready to go to recess when they had their library book out on their desk and everything else put away. As students returned from recess you reminded them to be self-starting on reading silently within one minute; 95% of the students were reading within one minute.

Polishers:

How might you help your students gain a clearer understanding of the proper procedures for getting out, using, and putting away math manipulatives?

Reproducible: Page 162, Appendix

the teacher is competent in the area of communicating immediate Expectations clearly and exemplary in communicating procedures for students to self-start on their work. However, Mr. Blair has not achieved competency in establishing and communicating clear procedures for using learning centers and handling math manipulatives and other hands-on materials properly.

A completed *Focused Observation Tool* can be used for debriefing with your teacher so you can point out the elements of Expectations performed well and one element on which to focus. We recommend principals give only one Polisher for each evaluation. This strategy identifies one specific aspect of Expectations to refine so the teacher can improve practice incrementally rather than being overwhelmed with several elements that demand radical changes.

The *Focused Observation Tool* is ideal to use during a 10– to 15–minute time period with your teacher to observe the use of Expectations. Note or describe specific examples of your teacher's proper uses of Expectations that clarify behaviors such as self-starting on work, raising hands, and waiting to be called on, or moving silently among centers. Look for evidence that your teacher has clarified Expectations for habitual procedures such as lining up, partner reading, signing up for individual conferences, and so forth.

Consulting in Greater Depth for Expectations

Another tool for collecting more in-depth data for working with teachers who struggle with Expectations is a *Depth Observation Tool*, like the one on this page, which is designed to make specific, descriptive notes about both immediate and habitual Expectations. The tool's purpose is to observe whether or not teachers have established and are reinforcing each type of Expectation.

Notice how Mr. Johnson's principal completed this tool. The teacher had established both immediate and habitual Expectations. For instance, students were expected to move silently and to work quietly, but Mr. Johnson had not set Expectations for what his students should do when they had completed their work. On the plus side, Mr. Johnson had reinforced students for moving quietly. Note that his principal used the 2nd column to document this along with the approximate percent of students on task. Mr. Johnson missed an opportunity for reinforcing students for working quietly during independent work, which his principal highlighted in the 3rd column with a question to trigger a discussion at a later date to encourage Mr. Johnson to develop concrete strategies. The principal also posed questions to prompt Mr. Johnson to communicate Expectations for students to meet when their work is completed.

Expectations Depth Observation Tool

Name: D. Johnson Date: 11/4/09
Grade/Subject: 4th Observer: J.Heinz

Directions: Describe student behaviors and procedures as they reflect teacher's Expectations and note missed opportunities

Expectations that are Established	Expectations that are Reinforced	Missed Opportunities
1. Silent movement with intent 2. Work quietly during independent work	1.Complimented Sam on moving quietly to the reference shelf	1. None 2. How might you draw attention to students working quietly? 3. How can you set Expectations for what students should do when work completed?
1. Raise hand and wait to be called on 2. Start self on work when first enter room	2. Used Positive cueing to notice 3 students who had self-started–95% engaged	1. How might you use positive Cueing to get students to avoid calling out answers?

Observation Notes:

Keepers:

1. You had set Expectations for silent movement with intent, work quietly during independent work time, raising hands, and self starting when entering room.
2. You used positive cueing to reinforce students who met the Expectations of moving silently and starting themselves on work.

Polishers:

1. How might you use positive cueing for reinforcing students who are conforming to each of your Expectations rather than just a few?
2. How might you set Expectations for what students should do when their work is completed?

Reproducible: Page 163, Appendix

An important caution: Even though the principal has noted several things the teacher might improve, the principal sets no more than one or two goals at a time to ensure focused advancement.

Other Strategies for Consulting about Expectations

Some teachers need to see evidence of Expectations working successfully in an actual classroom situation before they can understand fully how to become more effective at implementing this skill. A struggling teacher may indeed gain a better understanding of Expectations strategies by participating with you in a demo observation of a teacher who uses them effectively.

Expectations Demo Observation Tool

Observer: *Jenny Table* Grade/Class: *3rd g. self-contained*
Demo Teacher: *Mrs. Shuling Woo* Date/Time: *10/18/09*

Directions: Describe specific student behaviors and procedures as they reflect teacher's Expectations. Then set a goal for transferring a strategy into instruction of your own

Immediate Expectations (Short Term)		Habitual Expectations (Long Term)	
Teacher Action	**Student Response**	**Teacher Action**	**Student Response**
1. T. set the expectation for S. to move silently when they went to the library and to leave personal space between themselves and others. *2. T. thanked Sam and Ray for respecting personal space and winked at Jon.*	*1. All S. but Jon moved quietly from their desks and lined up leaving personal space.* *2. Sam and Ray smiled, and Jon immediately gave more space to the student in front of him.*	*1. Prior to s recess, the t. had them reread the self-starting chart and imagine self-start upon returning.* *2. Prior to starting small group reading instruction, t. reviewed the procedure for using new learning center. She focused on getting out, using, and putting materials away.* *3. T. redirected two s. to use the learning center materials appropriately.*	*1. After recess break, 90% of s. started themselves on a five-problem math quiz within one minute of returning to class.* *2. All but two s. who used the learning center were careful to use the materials appropriately then put them away correctly. Two s. goofed off with the materials.* *The two students responded to the redirection by stopping their goof-offs and using the materials constructively.*

Teacher Transfer: In my classroom, I want to set and refine this Expectation:
I want to teach students the self-starting procedure using the four-step process of telling, showing, practicing, and refining.

Reproducible: Page 164, Appendix

As part of a demo observation, you might use a *Demo Observation Tool* like the one to the left. This tool demonstrates consulting between a principal and Jenny Table, a new teacher who was struggling with setting and refining Expectations. Together, the principal and Ms. Table observed Mrs. Woo who was known to set and maintain Expectations masterfully.

Prior to the observation, the principal held a pre-conference with Jenny to introduce her to the demo observation process and to the tool she and the principal would use to make notes. Then they observed Mrs. Woo. Jenny's principal remained for part of the time, casually checking Jenny's notes during the observation, but Jenny remained for three hours including a recess break. This amount of time gave Jenny a chance to observe Mrs. Woo use Expectations in a variety of situations such as students moving to the library, leaving and returning from recess break, and using learning centers during small group instruction. On the tool, you can see Jenny Table's observations including a "Teacher Transfer" goal, which is an important outcome of consulting.

After Jenny completed the observation, her principal reviewed the data they both collected and worked with Jenny to identify one specific Expectation to incorporate into her classroom practice. Jenny chose to introduce the self-starting procedure because she saw that students became engaged immediately on productive work in Mrs. Woo's class rather than losing time to unnecessary behavior problems, the kinds that had been occurring in Jenny's classroom after recess breaks. The principal planned with Jenny how she might use the four-step process for teaching Expectations to ensure that (1) students will clearly understand the self-starting procedure and (2) students will feel an obligation to follow their teacher's Expectations.

A variation of the demo observation might have been to ask Mrs. Woo to set and refine Expectations with Jenny's students—in Jenny's classroom—while Jenny participates, or "collaborates." This approach works best when both teachers—in this case, Jenny and Mrs. Woo—have established rapport with each other and with Jenny's students. In short, you should use your judgment before deciding that this approach will yield success. If it does work, this kind of demonstration may help your teacher immeasurably, particularly in learning to tailor Expectations with precision while gaining insight into strategies another teacher uses.

Shadow Your Teacher for Expectations

Similar to the way parents support their young toddlers by holding their hands to transition from crawling to walking on their own, shadowing is a means by which you can give your teacher real-time guided practice in setting up and refining Expectations with students. This technique allows you to guide your teacher through the four-step process for setting up a classroom Expectation. For instance, your teacher can take students through the process while you intervene, as needed, to help make each step effective. Such interventions may help your teacher remember what should occur at each step, perhaps even providing verbiage that helps present concepts or that helps facilitate a teacher-student *Looks Like/Sounds Like* discussion.

To prepare a shadowing session, schedule a 10– to 15–minute time when your teacher will use the four-step process to teach a new Expectation to students. During this session, position yourself to the side of the action or toward the rear of the room, but not too far away. As needed, you may cross behind your teacher to whisper suggestions for phrasing concepts or for completing one step and moving to the next. For instance, if your teacher spends too much time on the *Looks Like/Sounds Like* chart in an effort to cover every aspect of an Expectation, you might whisper, *"Move on to the next step of demonstrating."*

In the next table, you will find some additional help using a gradual release technique for shadowing your teacher. You will notice that these suggested directions are grouped into three types: *Directing* tells your teacher exactly what to say; *Guiding* directs or leads your teacher to focus his or her own actions; and *Signaling* provides Signals that you offer your teacher from the side or back of the room. The table is designed to show shadowing with a teacher who is working on using the four steps of teaching the habitual (long-term) Expectation of students starting themselves on work when they first enter the room.

Shadowing for Expectations		
Gradual Release	**Directing:** Tell the teacher exactly what to say.	Say, *"Today, I am going to teach you a habit that will help you become a very successful student."* Say, *"Students, what would it look like and sound like if all students in this classroom came in quietly and started themselves on work?"* Say, *"Students, watch to see what Tom and Hilda do right and what they could refine as they model self-starting."*
	Guiding: Ask the teacher questions that will guide him/her to focus.	*"How might you set up the guided practice to have students self-start the correct way?"* *"How might you help students see what they did well during their first practice of self-starting?"* *"How might you help ________ self-start on a quiz?"*
	Signaling: From the back of the room, Cue the teacher.	Silently snap fingers—(Move to the next step.) Write in the air—(Chart students' ideas.) Walk fingers along arm, then touch heart—(Walk around the room and whisper compliments to students who have self-started correctly.)

Coaching for Expectations

Remember: Consultations and debriefings normally follow your observation visits, but coaching efforts *must precede and follow classroom observation visits*. Once your teacher has a basic understanding of engagement strategies for Expectations, he or she is ready to take more responsibility for anticipating which Expectations are needed and when, and to help students maintain them during a lesson (Glickman, et al, 2004; Lipton, et al, 2001; Zepeda, 2007a, 2007b). In your coaching stance for Expectations, help your teacher think through *and plan for* specific opportunities that may present themselves in the next lesson that you will observe. Such a conversation enhances your teacher's innate understanding of the nature of Expectations and may increase your teacher's success in developing this foundational skill.

A useful coaching strategy is to have your teacher visualize presenting the lesson to the students. Most important, have your teacher mentally practice how to use and maintain the Expectations. This mental exercise can increase the likelihood that your teacher will recall the plan and implement it correctly. Visualizing is one of the most effective ways you can help your teacher make setting and maintaining Expectations a natural part of teaching style. It adds only a few minutes to one of your coaching meetings.

The key to the coaching stance is engaging your teacher in one or more pre-observation dialogues to help the teacher anticipate situations that will require—possibly challenge—his or her current level of development with Expectations. Help this teacher identify places in the upcoming lesson that will require conscious efforts to employ Expectations. Remember that in your coaching stance, your role is not to dictate or supply strategies, but rather to elicit and discuss whatever tactics your teacher can suggest. Following are some questions you can use to encourage and assist the teacher in unlocking his or her own thinking.

Coaching Conversation for Expectations
Questions for Planning a Visit and Observation

- What is your Expectation goal during your lesson?
- Walk me through your lesson. What opportunities do you see at each step for using immediate and habitual Expectations?
- What behavioral problems do you foresee? How can you use Expectations to preempt these possible situations?
- What will you see that will Cue you to refocus your use of Expectations?
- How will you know if your use of Expectations is successful?

When following up with your teacher after the coaching observation, encourage a reflective type of conversation focused on helping your teacher identify insights and goals for strategies to integrate into classroom practice. At the end of this conversation, help your teacher identify one aspect or strategy of Expectations to address consciously in moving forward.

Here are some questions you might use to facilitate such a dialogue. Consider providing your teacher with your observation data prior to this conversation:

Reflective Conversation Questions
Following the Visit and Observation

- How did it go? Did you meet your Expectations goal? How do you know?
- Did your plans to use Expectations go as planned? Why or why not?
- What patterns do you see in the data I shared with you?
- What does this data tell you about your uses of Expectations?
- What did you learn about the use of Expectations that you want to replicate?
- What ONE thing do you want to refine to enhance your use of Expectations?

Chapter 5

Attention Prompts

Skill #2

The Big Eight Engagement Skills

EXPECTATIONS

Attention Prompts
Teacher uses verbal or visual prompts to focus students' attention for instruction to follow.

PROXIMITY

CUEING

SIGNALS

TIME LIMITS

TASKING

VOICE

5

Attention Prompts

Skill #2

TOOLS for Evaluating ATTENTION PROMPTS

See Appendix pp. 165–166

CASE STUDY

Sandra's successful first year teaching 6th grade math left her and her principal confident that Sandra had real talent. Her students gave her their Attention unfailingly, they appeared to like her, and they worked diligently all year-long, so it was natural for Sandra to assume her next year's students would respond the same way

By the third week of Sandra's second school year, her principal noticed persistent loud noise from Sandra's room, so she decided to observe informally from the hallway. What Mrs. Beaumont noticed was Sandra "teaching from your desk," as she later observed to her teacher. Rather than using Attention Prompts like:

> *Students, may I have your Attention now [pause for 3 seconds with eye contact]* OR *Josh has his eyes on me* OR *table 3 is very focused,*

Sandra began her lessons when *she* was ready, whether or not her students were attentive.

"I have a tough group of kids this year," Sandra complained.

As she began consulting with Sandra, Mrs. Beaumont arranged for her teacher to visit other classrooms specifically to

Think of this engagement skill—**Attention Prompts**—as a strategy that communicates STOP and FOCUS to all students. Even the very best teachers have faced classes that defy control, at least at the beginning of the year, and a teacher may feel like a fire whistle or boat horn will be the only way to guarantee Attention. Successful teachers find ways of ensuring Attention, although not always at first and sometimes through practice and reinforcement—but never with horns and whistles.

On the other hand, some teachers struggle all year long to catch children's Attention—some assuming that when they stand up in the front of the room and begin talking, students will stop what they are doing and listen. Unfortunately, this is seldom enough; it is merely an Expectation without a strategy.

As you know, failure to capture students' Attention results in students failing to receive critical information.

Keep in mind that an *Attention Prompt* is a teacher's way of indicating a major break, an important change in the action of the classroom. As you observe, identify your teacher's technique(s) for gaining students' Attention—not only at the beginning of class but also during the course of instruction. *How* does your teacher get students to understand directions, Expectations, instruction, or redirection? Look to see how many children respond and note *how* they respond. Your basic rule of thumb should be this: ***Teacher talks only when students are listening*** (Gudmundsen, et. al, 1996).

This chapter focuses on recognizing effective Attention Prompts and helping teachers develop this crucial skill.

> CASE STUDY – *cont'd*
>
> observe for successful methods of prompting Attention.
>
> Sandra used a *Focused Observation Tool* to list tactics the other teachers used for prompting Attention and for Cueing their Expectations. Then she outlined the pattern of a good Attention Prompt that she would like to try on her own:
>
> 1. Whisper to off-task students, e.g., *Attention in one minute* OR *I can't wait to see who comes first to Attention!*
> 2. Deliver Attention Prompt, e.g., *Class, Attention in 5. . .*
> 3. Pause for 3 to 4 seconds and make eye contact.
> 4. Offer positive Cues. e.g., *Tim has eyes on me* OR *Anne has her lab manual open.*
> 5. Begin teaching the lesson. Use Proximity as necessary.
>
> With her principal's help, Sandra recognized that her choice of a specific Attention Prompt would not be as important as actually *using* a prompt. They debriefed about next steps: (1) follow a pattern of prompts for Attention, and (2) teach the "habit" of Attention so students will learn what Attention looks and sounds like.
>
> This chapter offers more detail about Mrs. Beaumont's consultations with Sandra, and the observation tools they used.
>
> 

Elements of Attention

As you observe for **Attention** strategies, you may find that some teachers have success with fairly simple, straightforward prompts. For instance, teachers of primary and intermediate grades sometimes repeat simple verbal prompts like "Class, eyes on me" to focus students' Attention, or else they might use a visual Cue like holding up a hand in a "Stop" gesture probably accompanied by a verbal Cue. Quite often middle-level teachers do not see the need for using Attention Prompts. They feel that at this age students simply should know better; they should have already been trained to be ready for instruction. Yet the simple truth is that even adults need Attention Prompts to mentally prepare for receiving information. Student learning will be greatly enhanced if teachers use a prompt to get students' Attention before beginning the lesson (Carnine, Silbert, Kame'enui, & Tarver, 2004). **Teachers who use Attention Prompts will probably have far fewer discipline problems and achieve higher levels of student learning. *The reason is obvious: Students focusing their listening are students learning how to learn.***

The prompt a teacher chooses to gain students' Attention should not be your focus. What should matter is the process your teacher uses once he or she has given the prompt. On the simplest level, the process you are looking for is the way your teacher combines elements; that is, since no *one* kind of prompt works in every situation, your teacher's process should blend verbal and visual elements and possibly musical ones.

Students of all ages benefit from Attention Prompts, particularly those that alert them to a change in focus. Naturally, an Attention Prompt in kindergarten will sound different from one in 9th grade biology. The kindergarten teacher may sound overly inviting, *"Boys and Girls, eyes and ears on me in 5 seconds.* (Pause to make eye contact.) *4. . .Emmanuel is looking at me. 3. . .Samuel has his listening ears on,"* and so forth. On the other hand, the biology teacher may sound more businesslike and may incorporate course details into a prompt, *"Ladies and Gentlemen, please focus your Attention now on the scalpel in my hand and the frog on my table.* (Pause to make eye contact.) *Your eyes forward tell me we are ready to begin. Thank you."*

Be alert for situations in which your teacher misses an opportunity to prompt for Attention. Some teachers, particularly inexperienced ones or those who have moved from elementary to secondary or vice versa, have an illusion that simply by beginning to speak they will catch students' Attention. You may need to work with your teacher to build this important skill and to recognize that using Attention Prompts whenever starting instruction or changing instructional focus can only increase engagement by making students ready to learn.

Following are Attention Prompts typically used in elementary classrooms.

Types of Attention Prompts	
Prompts	**Examples**
Verbal Prompts	*"Class, may I have your attention now."* *"Give me five."* *"One, two, three. . .eyes on me."* Students respond, *"One, two. . .eyes on you."*
Musical Prompts	Rain stick Chimes Train whistle Rhythm: Teacher claps a rhythm, students repeat
Visual Prompts	Teacher holds her hand up Teacher moves to a specific spot

Students in grades 6 and higher may respond best to prompts their teachers develop as part of establishing rapport early in the year. For instance, your 8th grade science teacher may have planted Attention Prompts during discussion of lab equipment and procedures during the first week of school. Perhaps the teacher explained that a prompt like holding and sounding a tuning fork would be his STOP prompt perhaps accompanied by a statement like "Heads up!" or "Time for whole-class focus." **Part of the teacher's process, of course, is building students' understanding that important information follows an Attention Prompt.**

You can learn much about your teacher's control of students' Attention during your observation visits or through simple "Drop-Ins." On the facing page is the *Drop-In Tool* Sandra's principal used before beginning their consultation about Attention Prompts (see Case Study this chapter). The data show that Sandra was deficient in utilizing Attention Prompts as well as Proximity (Chapter 6) for maintaining Attention. In addition, and perhaps most significant to the principal, the data revealed Sandra did not use prompts to focus Attention on instruction.

Notice that the principal identifies specific Keepers and one Polisher for this teacher's focus. In addition, the principal leaves behind a *Reflection Follow-Up Card* to serve as a feedback device for defining next steps. As you learned in Chapter 2, the principal should keep the *Drop-In Tool* as a record of the visit, which could be used later to demonstrate patterns and growth. The *Reflection Follow-Up Card* is the leave-behind—very important for the teacher's knowledge and for the teacher to celebrate growth.

Attention Prompts

Teachers rarely have trouble finding words to communicate their Expectations. Good teachers build a simple yet flexible process with their students to focus their Attention. Usually the Attention process combines types of Cues—verbal and visual Cues, for instance—in a pattern students come to know well. Good teachers build this process from day one with a class.

Example 1: Kindergarten

During a *Drop-In,* Mrs. Smith's kindergarten students are working independently in centers. The teacher finishes her last leveled reading group and prepares for the Attention Prompt. The principal observes her process, as follows:

Mrs. Smith moves about and whispers to each group of students, *"One minute until the train whistle."* During the timed minute, Mrs. Smith uses Proximity (Chapter 6) to whisper to certain students: "*Table 1 is already cleaned up. They will be ready for the Attention Prompt.*" She also whispers, "*Wow! Look at table 3—their eyes are already on me!*"

Drop-In Tool

Name: *Sandra Jones* Date/Time: *10/3/09, 9:00am*
Grade/Subject: *6th grade/math* Observer: *Ms. Beaumont*

Rating System:

✓+ = Strategy exceptionally well done
✓ = Strategy apparent and competent
✓– = Strategy attempted, not effective
– = Strategy missing, should occur

Physical Environment: (Domain III. Learning Environment):

✓ Student work is on display and clearly demonstrates the objective
✓– Student Expectations for behavior are posted
✓ Room is organized with easy access to materials
✓– Room arrangement lends itself to physical movement
✓ Learning objective is posted
✓– Schedule is posted

Classroom Management/Engagement: (Domain III. Learning Environment):

✓– Students know what to do and when and how to do it (EXPECTATIONS)
– Teacher uses prompts to focus instruction to follow (ATTENTION)
– Teacher moves purposefully around the classroom (PROXIMITY)
✓– Teacher uses positive, effective verbal Cues (CUEING)
✓– Teacher uses nonverbal Signals to direct students (SIGNALS)
✓– Teacher offers times for beginning and ending tasks (TIME LIMITS)
✓– Teacher sharpens engagement through questioning strategies (TASKING)
✓– Teacher uses positive, clear, effective tone and verbiage (VOICE)

Student Engagement: (Domain III. Learning Environment): 25 # students

Approximate PERCENTAGE of student engagement: *30-50%*
Students are engaged in work directly related to the objective. ✓ YES ___ NO

Comments/Questions: *K: Leaning objective is posted. Room is organized. What prompt could you use to get students' sttention before instructing?*

Follow-Up: *Do a 20-minute engagement observation for attention prompts.*

Reproducible: Page 153, Appendix

Example 2: 3rd Grade

During a consultation, Mrs. Mitchell's principal noted the high level of on-task behavior in her class (more than 90% at all times) and praised the efficient way students moved about her classroom, which was set up for cooperative groups. After Mrs. Mitchell explained how she manages Attention in her classroom, her principal asked her to list the steps in her process so they could share it with others. Her outline follows on the next page.

Process for Managing Attention in Classroom Mrs. Mitchell's Steps	
Step 1	Select a verbal Cue (and consider combining with a visual or musical Cue if you feel students need concrete reinforcement).
Step 2	Practice, or be sure to use, this Cue daily including your start-up process for beginning class.
Step 3	While students are working independently or in small groups, whisper a one-minute warning Cue such as *"Attention in one minute."* (Use Proximity by positioning yourself in the center of student activity rather than giving the Cue from your desk.)
Step 4	Get into your teaching position: gather and organize lesson materials, move into your teaching zone.
Step 5	Give the Attention Prompt, such as *"Class, may I have your Attention now."*
Step 6	Make eye contact with students by scanning their faces. Pause as you do this, perhaps 5 seconds.
Step 7	Offer two positive Cues, such as *"Thank you, Ellen, for having your eyes on me"* or *"Table 3 has their materials ready."*

Mrs. Smith then moves to the front of the room where she stands and blows the train whistle. She pauses for three seconds to make eye contact and then gives two more positive Cues. *"Look at Samuel. His eyes are on me and he is sitting in his chair"* and *"WOW! I see Bob looking at me!"* Chad, however, is not properly focused, so as Mrs. Smith begins the lesson, she moves toward Chad and offers him an expectant look (Proximity), Chad focuses his Attention. Mrs. Smith's principal places a check-plus for **Attention Prompts** on the *Drop-In Tool.*

Example 3: 7th Grade Math

Mr. Jeffries is ready to transition from a daily self-starter, or bell-ringer activity, into a direct instruction math lesson. He walks quickly around the perimeter of the room and whispers to students, *"In 30 seconds I will ask you to focus on me at the front."* Later, in consultation with his principal, Mr. Jeffries explained that he trained students from the first day to recognize different forms of focusing, *"We talked about the difference between focusing on a book, focusing on a group task, and focusing on a teacher or lecturer. The word 'focus' became my Attention Prompt."*

His principal also noted that Mr. Jeffries reliably begins math lessons with all students focused on instruction. Mr. Jeffries took his teaching position at the front of the room and announced, *"Class, Attention in 5."* He paused for three seconds making eye contact and then began the count-down while using positive Cues: *"5 Jenna has her starter put away. 4. . .Table 4 is focused and ready for math. Excellent! I don't even have to say 3. . .2. . .1."*

Recognizing Missed Opportunities

Be alert for classroom situations where students appear not fully engaged immediately after instruction or other learning activity has begun. The problem at such a moment may be a failure in using Attention Prompts or, worse, a failure to develop an ongoing, consistent process that students recognize—one that communicates STOP and FOCUS.

Nearly every teacher knows how to ask for Attention. Theoretically, it's as easy as hailing a cab or ordering iced tea. We know that problems arise when Attention Prompts are not introduced and reinforced, so training students in an Attention process should begin during the first days of school (Expectations). This doesn't always happen, so you the observer may notice that some Attention Prompts *sound* like Attention Prompts but somehow they don't seem to work very well. That's because (1) Attention as a process may not have been introduced and practiced, or (2) Attention Prompts may be confusing or poorly delivered. Here are some red flags (ineffective ***elements*** of Attention Prompts) buried inside Attention Prompts that don't work well:

Recognizing and Improving Weak Attention Prompts

Weak Attention Prompts	Ineffective Elements	Improvement
"Class, may I have your Attention. . . . Where did I put that test?" [Pause.] "CLASS, I ASKED FOR YOUR ATTENTION"	Teacher asks for students' Attention before being ready to teach. Making them wait after getting their Attention gives students permission to continue in off-task activities until they are sure the teacher is ready.	Before asking for Attention, get instructional materials ready and begin teaching immediately after students have given their Attention. **Don't ask for students' Attention until you are ready to teach**.
"Class, may I have your Attention nowletmetellyou what we are going to do today, , , ."	Similar to rolling through a stop sign, the teacher does not give students a chance to stop what they are doing to give their Attention. They may be merely processing the request when the teacher starts teaching.	When requesting students' Attention, pause for three seconds, look about, make eye contact, give positive Cues to students who have given Attention to focus the stragglers. Begin teaching immediately.
"Class, may I have your Attention now." (Teacher pauses to make eye contact). *"Josh has his eyes on me. Samantha has her book out and is ready to learn!"* OK (said in a higher voice).	All is fine until the end of the Prompt when teacher says, "OK!" in a high voice. This may release students from giving Attention and excuse them to misbehave.	After successfully gaining students' Attention, avoid using the word "OK!" Begin teaching in a well-modulated, expert voice.

(continued)

Recognizing and Improving Weak Attention Prompts		
Weak Attention Prompts	**Ineffective Elements**	**Improvement**
Students are working in cooperative groups with a significant amount of on-task noise. The teacher walks to the front of the room and gives an Attention Prompt.	Teacher fails to give students a heads up that a change is about to occur. Thus, students are not able to bring their collaborative activities to a close to prepare for the shift.	Teacher needs to use Proximity group to group to give a warning that an Attention Prompt is coming. When the prompt is given, students will be able to focus immediately.

Consulting for Attention Prompts

Attention is only one of the engagement behaviors you will observe and evaluate. The elements of Attention Prompts are both verbal and physical behaviors performed by the teacher. These Prompts impact student behavior, naturally, and spotting certain student behaviors will help you identify strengths and weaknesses in the teacher's mastery of Attention Prompts. It is unlikely, perhaps impossible, to find a classroom of engaged students without observing an effective Attention Prompt. **Your teacher must first *have* students' Attention to *keep* their attention.**

Reflection Follow-Up

Name: *Sandra Jones* Date: *10/15/09*
Grade/Subject: *6th math* Observer: *Ms. Beaumont*

Keepers: *Learning objective is posted. Room is well organized.*

Polishers: *What prompt could you use to get students' attention before you start instruction?*

Reproducible: Page 154, Appendix

Here is the *Reflection Follow-Up* left behind with Sandra Jones (see Case Study, this chapter). Offering your teacher a *Reflection Follow-Up* is a timely way to communicate the pluses (Keepers) and minuses (Polishers) you observed during the visit, and it helps prepare for the consultations to follow. Always remember to phrase the Polisher as a question so that you remain true to your consulting stance.

Once you have begun the process of consulting with your teacher regarding Attention Prompts, assist your teacher in thinking more deeply about this engagement skill. To do so, you may decide to collect additional data and, for that, we recommend a *Focused Observation Tool* for Attention, like the one on the facing page. In this next model, you will see a principal's evaluation and observation notes finding this teacher is competent in all but one area of warning that an Attention Prompt is coming, yet exceptional (✓+) in using Attention steps.

Point out the elements of Attention performed well, and identify one element to focus on. In this case, the principal notes only one Polisher so that the teacher has a specific, do-able, and deliberate focus for moving forward. We recommend noting only one Polisher per evaluation to ensure continual small growth steps and to avoid a teacher feeling overwhelmed or defeated.

To use this observation tool to focus on Attention, you should schedule a 5–minute time period when the teacher knows you will be watching for this engagement skill. During your observation, tally the teacher's successful uses of Attention on the tool.

At the conclusion of the observation, leave the teacher with a *Reflection Follow-Up* that identifies Keepers and Polishers.

Attention Prompts
Focused Observation Tool

Name: T. Williams Date: 10/3/09
Grade/Subject: 1st Observer: T. Long

Directions: Observe student behaviors and procedures as they reflect teacher's Expectations.

✓ = Competent example of Attention Prompts
✓+ = Excellent example of Attention Prompts
✓– = Ineffective attempt of Attention Prompts

The teacher . . .

–	gives student a warning that an Attention Prompt is coming
✓	uses an Attention Prompt before instructing
✓	is in the teacher position and ready to instruct
✓	uses a credible voice
✓+	Prompt Steps ____ prompts ____ pauses for 2 to 3 seconds making eye contact ____ gives two positive Cues ____ begins teaching immediately

Observation Notes:

Keepers:
You used all of the prompt steps effectively. 95% of students responded to your Attention Prompt. You used Proximity to bring in Sam.

Polishers:
Polishers: How could you warn students that an Attention Prompt is coming?

Reproducible: Page 165, Appendix

Other Strategies for Consulting about Attention Prompts

To help a teacher gain a better understanding or to help a teacher recognize specific tactics and strategies for employing Attention Prompts in the classroom, you might consider the following options:

Option 1: Guide Your Teacher through a Demo Observation.

Arrange for your teacher to observe several teachers who demonstrate mastery of Attention in their daily teaching. Have your teacher use a simple tool like the one that follows for this observation in order to (1) identify specific uses of Attention Prompts by the demonstration teacher, (2) enter a brief description of each use of Attention Prompts according to its element: *prompt, pause for 2 to 3 seconds making eye contact, give two positive Cues, begin teaching immediately,* and (3) note the student response for each teacher action. In your debriefing, be sure to ask your teacher not only to identify each use of Attention Prompts by the demonstration teacher, but also to describe the resulting effects of each prompt upon student behavior. In addition, help your teacher set one or two goals for whichever elements of Attention you think the teacher should transfer into classroom practice.

Here is an example of a completed *Demo Observation Tool*. In this example, Sandra Jones and her administrator have observed Mrs. Cole's 4th grade class.

Attention Prompts Demo Observation Tool

Observer: Jones/Beaumont Grade/Class: 4th, self-contained
Demo Teacher: Mrs. Helen Cole Date/Time: 10/15/09

Directions: Describe specific Attention Prompts as they reflect teacher's Expectations, and describe specific student responses to those prompts.

Prompt		Pause Making Eye Contact		Positive Cues	
Teacher Action	**Student Response**	**Teacher Action**	**Student Response**	**Teacher Action**	**Student Response**
Teacher goes to each group of students warning them that the prompt is in 30 seconds.	Begin cleaning up and moving to seats.	Teacher makes eye contact; gives "the teacher look" to the two students who are not focused.	Students sit up straight and focus on Mrs. Cole.	"Thank you, table 3, for having your materials put away." "Erin's attention is on me."	All but one student settle into focused Attention.
"Class, attention in 5."	80% of students stop action and focus on Mrs. Cole.			Mrs. Cole begins the math lesson while moving toward Bob (unfocused) She whispers to Bob to see her at recess. (She plans to practice Attention Prompts with Bob at recess.)	

Teacher Transfer: In my classroom, I want to set and refine this use of Attention:

1. When making eye contact, focus specific eye contact on those students who are not responding.
2. Give positive cues that are specific.

Reproducible: Page 166, Appendix

Option 2: Shadow Your Teacher for Attention Prompts.

Shadowing is a technique for providing real-time guided practice for the teacher while intervening as needed to identify opportunities for applying specific Attention strategies.

To arrange for shadowing, schedule a 5–minute time period with your teacher when he or she will be transitioning, which requires an Attention Prompt. Stand to one side of the room.

Cross behind the teacher as you see fit so that you can offer informational Cues such as *"Make eye contact with Bob"* or *"Tell table 3 what they are doing correctly."* You can offer specific directions like *"Take the teacher stance," "Use a credible voice,"* or *"Give a warning that the Attention Prompt is coming."*

As your teacher responds to your guidance, you can switch to using observer Signals from a greater distance like from the back of the room. In advance of a shadowing session, you may identify Signals like these:

Shadowing for Attention Prompts

Signal	Indication
Fingers making a circle	Move around the classroom and warn students that an Attention Prompt is coming
Point to the front of the room	Move to the front before giving the Attention Prompt
Point to your eyes	Make eye contact with individuals
Thumbs up	Give positive Cues

Coaching for Attention Prompts

While your consultations and debriefings will follow your observation visits, your coaching efforts must precede and follow visits designed to further apply and practice skill development once your teacher has a basic understanding of Attention Prompts (Glickman, et al, 2004; Lipton, et al, 2001; Zepeda, 2007a, 2007b).

In your coaching stance regarding Attention, help your teacher think through specific opportunities that may present themselves in the next lesson that you will observe. This conversation before a lesson will greatly enhance your teacher's innate understanding and appreciation of Attention Prompts and will increase the teacher's success with this skill. Mentally practicing planned behaviors in an upcoming lesson may increase the likelihood that your teacher will recall the plan and implement it correctly.

The key to the coaching stance is engaging in one or more pre-observation dialogues to help your teacher anticipate situations that will not only require, but also might challenge, his or her current state of Attention Prompt skill development (Glickman, et al, 2004; Lipton, et al, 2001; Zepeda, 2007a, 2007b).

Help the teacher identify transitions and other points in an upcoming lesson that will require conscious efforts to employ Attention Prompts. Remember that in your coaching stance, your role is to elicit and discuss whatever tactics your teacher can suggest (Glickman, et al, 2004; Lipton, et al, 2001; Zepeda, 2007a, 2007b). These may include possible timing of Attention Prompts as well as the steps in an Attention Prompt. Here are questions you can use:

Coaching Conversation for Attention Prompts Questions for Planning a Visit and Observation

- What is your Attention goal during your lesson?
- Walk me through a lesson. What opportunities do you see for using Attention Prompts?
- What behavioral problems do you foresee? How can you use Attention Prompts to curtail these possible situations?
- What will you see that will alert you to refocus your Attention Prompt?
- How will you know if your Attention Prompts are successful?

After the observation, when following up with your teacher, encourage a reflective type of conversation that will help the teacher cement what he or she did well so that these positive skill behaviors—these new skill applications—can be repeated. This conversation also presents an opportunity for the teacher to identify—with you—one element to consciously address in moving forward to refine Attention Prompts. Here are some questions you might use:

Reflective Conversation Questions Following the Visit and Observation

- How did it go? Did you meet your goal with Attention Prompts? How do you know?
- Did your strategies to use Attention Prompts go as planned? Why or why not?
- What patterns do you see in the data I shared with you?
- What does this data tell you about your uses of Attention Prompts?
- What did you learn about Attention Prompts that you want to replicate?
- What ONE thing do you want to refine further in your use of Attention Prompts?

Chapter 6

Proximity

Skill #3

The Big Eight Engagement Skills

EXPECTATIONS
ATTENTION PROMPTS
Proximity Teacher moves purposefully around the classroom for maximum effect.
CUEING
SIGNALS
TIME LIMITS
TASKING
VOICE

6

Proximity

Skill #3

TOOLS for Evaluating PROXIMITY

See Appendix pp. 167–171

Proximity is not only a matter of positioning oneself in the classroom, but also a matter of communicating with students via eye contact, posture, movement around the classroom, and any other body language from the teacher to deliver constructive information.

To most children, the classroom teacher is figuratively the 800–pound gorilla in the room having potential to wield enormous power, so ***physicality*** is an important element of each teacher's communication system. **To use *Proximity* effectively, a teacher needs "with-it-ness," a state described by Kounin (1970) as a heightened sense of awareness of *what is happening* or *what is about to happen* in the classroom, and the research suggests that children draw meaning from physicality at an even greater rate, nearly two-to-one, than from verbal expression.**

Communication of Meaning Proportion of meaning inferred from nonverbal and verbal components	
65% from Nonverbal Components	35% Verbal Components
Posture	Pitch
Gesture	Volume
Proximity	Inflection
Muscle tension	Pace
Facial expression	Words

Source: Burgoon, J. K., Buller, D. B., & Woodall, W. G. (1989). *Nonverbal communication: The unspoken dialogue*. New York: Harper and Row.

From day one in most classes, every child is ready to—and many are eager to—receive direction in every way possible. Kids like to know what is expected of them, so each

Elements of Proximity

Teachers who use Proximity to great advantage may also be teachers who organize their classrooms carefully. A teacher who masters his or her own environment is well suited to feel and act comfortably in that setting and to position himself or herself strategically and dynamically. Why is this important? For one reason, classrooms that are well structured encourage and facilitate on-task behavior by students (Morrison, 1979) and more positive behavior generally. **Beyond their organization of the learning environment, teachers who use Proximity well are those who supervise and facilitate the learning process actively. These are the teachers who move about, look in all directions, interact simultaneously with individuals and small groups and whole-class groups, and who observe and comment, correct and redirect as necessary—sometimes, seemingly, all at once** (Colvin, et al, 1997; De Pry & Sugai, 2002; Johnson, et al, 1996).

At some time in our lives as students, we all have been taught by teachers who mastered Proximity. You may not have to search your memory very hard to recall one or two excellent examples. Yet, at the time, you probably were not consciously aware of the teacher's skill. When Proximity is performed well, it appears natural, almost effortless.

Bring those memories with you into your classroom observations, and look for the hallmarks of successful, effective Proximity. Identify the aspects of your teacher's physicality that you think speak the loudest to students, and consider the following as you observe and evaluate that performance:

Elements of Proximity		
Element of Proximity	**Lack of Proximity**	**Effective Proximity**
Positioning (Location in the classroom) (**Non-Positioning** results from teacher out of Proximity)	Teacher remains stationary at desk or in front of the room during instruction or group work.	*Teacher moves with intent around the classroom in anticipation of student needs and/or problems.*
Visual Scanning (Eye-to-eye contact)	Teacher focuses on material such as textbook, overhead, or elements other than student engagement, including turning away from students frequently.	*Teacher's visual gaze scans faces of all students with regularity and with intent to monitor their attention and to elicit interactions.*
Presence (Posture/poise)	Teacher exhibits hesitancy, frustration, disorganization, fear, lack of preparation, and general lack of command.	*Teacher communicates expertise and authority through body language such as confident posture, purposeful gestures, and credible tone of voice.*

It may be important for you, the evaluator, to distinguish effective Proximity from mere *wandering*. The teacher who wanders may achieve short-lived effects such as squelching random off-task behavior, but the wandering teacher soon discovers that students' behavior quickly veers again off-task or else doesn't change at all. When you observe a teacher who appears to "put out fires" that restart, you are observing ineffective Proximity.

Remember that effective Proximity is a direct correlation between teacher physicality and student engagement, and keep in mind that physicality encompasses physical location, body language, and eye contact.

On page 70 is a *Time-on-Task Tool* from an observation revealing several skill weaknesses: (1) multiple engagement skills appear lacking or weak, (2) significant weaknesses appear to be Proximity and Cueing (Chapter 7), and (3) Proximity may be the first skill to address because it heightens the teacher's presence, serves as a catalyst to motivate students to stay on task, and reduces the tendencies of some to misbehave. The data shows Cueing may not be effective until this teacher uses Proximity.

Recognizing Successful Uses of Proximity

> CASE STUDY
>
> Rob Selig didn't need his principal to tell him his 4th graders had become harder for him to manage during the past five years. Rob blamed changes in population, as his school had been designated Title I with increasing numbers at-risk.
>
> Rob's principal shared his *Time-on-Task Tool* that revealed a marked decrease in Attention (50% down to 21%) when Rob stood at his desk to direct or reprimand off-task students for not meeting the Expectation to self-start.
>
> Rob and his principal devised a plan: Through a process of consulting and coaching, Rob would follow these steps in using Proximity for self-starting:
>
> 1. Greet students at the door to remind them to self-start.
> 2. Move to back of the room to observe students begin work.
> 3. Then move about the room, positioning close to students most likely to digress.
> 4. Circulate but return to all possible trouble spots, scan the room continually, make eye contact as needed.

Teachers who exhibit *proximital intent*, or purposeful presence, use their physicality to influence student awareness and behavior, and often they do this consciously (Colvin, et al, 1997; De Pry & Sugai, 2002). **A teacher's repertoire may include not only strategic placements amid the crosscurrents of student interaction, but also may include behavior reinforcements like verbal and nonverbal Cues to signal to students—individually or collectively—that their behavior is appropriate.**

Example 1: 5th Grade Math Lesson

During her lesson on fractions, Mrs. Martland ***continually scans*** and ***rescans*** the faces of her students to note which ones are engaged and which ones are faltering in their Attention to the subject at hand. As she ***turns toward*** and ***away from*** the whiteboard, she notices two boys having a side conversation. Although she recognizes that the conversation is quiet and non-interruptive, Mrs. Martland ***pauses***, creating a moment of silence in the classroom, and ***fixes her gaze*** pleasantly but deliberately on the boys until one and then the other ***makes eye contact*** with her. They stop talking, and Mrs. Martland gives them a quick smile as she continues to address the whole class. In follow-up discussion, this teacher remarked to her principal that had the two boys resumed their conversation, she would have moved closer to their desks—perhaps in position to look down squarely at them—so that her physical repositioning would communicate that further action such as a reprimand from her would be forthcoming.

Example 2: 8th Grade Writing Group

Mr. Kilroy's class is set up with three groups on this Friday afternoon to brainstorm topics for essays they will write about a novel they have been reading. As he sits and talks with Group A, Mr. Kilroy's head turns regularly toward each of the other groups. At one point, he catches the eyes of a boy in Group C who is returning to his group after pulling a dictionary from a shelf. Mr. Kilroy gives the boy a thumbs-up to reinforce two things: (1) He is aware of how each child is performing even when he is at a distance, and (2) he recognizes and approves of this boy's behavior. In follow-up discussion with his principal, this teacher discussed Group B, the loudest of the three, and decided that next time he would stand closer more frequently to that group to help keep their volume down. Mr. Kilroy added that next time he would offer positive Cues (Chapter 7) to groups with appropriate noise levels: e.g., *"Group A is using a whisper voice. Excellent!"* If Group B, on the other hand, is still too loud, Mr. Kilroy would offer verbal reminders to be aware of the impact of their volume on other groups.

Example 3: 2nd Grade Reading Cluster

Ms. Appleby's reading group sits clustered around their teacher on a rug. Eloise, at the back of the group, sits half-turned toward her friend. More than once, Eloise looks from her friend's face to her teacher's until Ms. Appleby shakes her head "No" at the girl. In follow-up discussion, this teacher acknowledged the advantage of combining of *visual Proximity* (deliberate eye contact) and *physical Proximity* (the head shake) to encourage this child's positive performance.

CASE STUDY – *cont'd*

Rob's principal made two more visits and recorded on-task behavior at 50% and then 65%. By a third visit, 80% of students were self-starting with more than 60% remaining engaged for the entire period. Proximity felt like magic to Rob.

In follow-up consultations a few weeks later, Rob suggested that on-task behavior was beginning to dip again with a few students remaining troublesome.

Again, his principal visited to observe self-starting and noted that Rob's use of physicality and visual scanning were having positive results even if engagement was declining somewhat. With his principal's suggestion and help, Rob decided to add positive Cueing by using a *Looks Like/Sounds Like* chart to teach the habit of self-starting (Expectations). Here is their chart:

Self-Starting (SS)

Looks Like

- Put stuff away
- Go right to seat
- Look at directions
- Get SS materials out
- Begin SS work immediately
- Work quietly

Sounds Like

- Quiet voices when enter room
- Silence of students not talking
- Soft whisper of pencils writing or pages turning

The chart helped Rob generate Cues like *Thank you, Eddie, for entering the room quietly* AND *I see that Mindy and Paul have gone to their seats with open books* AND *I am very impressed with table 2's head start.*

As Rob took more responsibility for improving student engagement, the principal shifted to a coaching stance and followed up with the *Focused Observation Tool* for Proximity you will find in this chapter. ♦♦♦

Time-On-Task (Observation Tool for All Engagement Skills)

Name: *Rob Selig* Date: *10/16/09* # Students: *24* Grade/Class: *4th* Observer: *Tawny Verhaal*

Directions: Record the time for each observation you make of educator involvement in learning. Record observations as follows:

1. Mark percentage of student engagement. (P) passive, (A) active
2. Describe teacher actions causing disengagement.
3. Describe relevant student behavior, especially off-task behavior.
4. Ask yourself, "What would I do if I were the teacher?"
5. Check recommended action(s)—those things that you would do if you were the teacher. You may also want to ★ actions that the teacher performs well.

FOR EACH INTERVAL, show % of Student Engagement.

WRITE **A** for alert, attentive behavior, or
P for passive, disengaged behavior. **THEN DESCRIBE**

INTERVALS	Teacher Actions Impacting Students (Below)	AND Student Engagement and Behavior (Below)	Expectations	Attention Prompts	Proximity	Cueing	Signals	Time Limits	Tasking	Voice
Interval No. 1	% Engaged: ___ 0–5% ___ 6–25% *A* 26–33%	___ 34–50% *P* 51–79% ___ 80–100%	X		X	X		X		X
8:25 am self-start	**Teacher Actions:** *Sitting at desk–back of room. From desk, "Be sure you self-start." Yelling – "Start your self-starter!"*	**Student Behavior:** *Entrance loud–5 on-task. 15 at desks, 8 working, 9 wandering 20 at desk, 18 working, 4 wandering*	X X		X X	X				
Interval No. 2	% Engaged: ___ 0–5% ___ 6–25% *A P* 26–33%	___ 34–50% ___ 51–79% ___ 80–100%	X		X	X				X
8:30 am self-start	**Teacher Actions:** *At desk, shouting names of 4 students. "Get to work." Teacher moves to the front of the room. "Stop and Listen! How many times do I have to say it–get to work, now!–back to seat!"*	**Student Behavior:** *4 to seat and work, 12 working, 4 side conversations, 4 rummaging in desks. All in desks–8 in side conversations (4 of the same), 5 rummaging, 1 head down, 6 working, 4 just sitting–noise raising.*	X			X				X
Interval No. 3	% Engaged: ___ 0–5% ___ 6–25% ___ 26–33%	*P* 34–50% *A* 51–79% ___ 80–100%	X	X		X		X		X
8:35 am transition	**Teacher Actions:** *"Stop and Listen! – If you don't want to work, you can complete your SS at recess. Get out your math books, turn to page 75."*	**Student Behavior:** *Students groan. Rummaging in desks for math books–talking, muttering.*				X				
Interval No. 4	% Engaged: ___ 0–5% ___ 6–25% *A* 26–33%	___ 34–50% *P* 51–79% ___ 80–100%								
8:38 am math direct ins.	**Teacher Actions:** *Starts teaching without looking up–writing on board with back to students.*	**Student Behavior:** *5 listening. 8 still trying to find page 75. 4 side conversations (same), 5 looking in desks, 2 at water fountain. Noise increasing.*	X			X			X	X
Interval No. 5	% Engaged: ___ 0–5% ___ 6–25% *A* 26–33%	___ 34–50% *P* 51–79% ___ 80–100%								
8:40 am Ind. practice	**Teacher Actions:** *Book down, hands on hips. "If you don't want to listen, figure it out yourself. Do all problems on page 76." Teacher returns to desk.*	**Student Behavior:** *6 rolling eyes, 7 working, 4 side conversations (same), 5 hands raised for help while chatting, 2 heads down.*	X		X	X		X	X	X

Recommended Actions:

1. *Greet students at the door and remind them to begin self-starting within 10 seconds.*
2. *Use proximity and whisper positive cues to students who are self-starting.*

Recognizing Missed Opportunities

Proximity may be one of the quickest fixes for a struggling teacher because it is a skill many can comprehend easily. When probed, teachers might recall seeing effective uses of Proximity from their own experiences as students, and if necessary, they may be able to recognize Proximity demonstrated by others in your school.

Be on the lookout for common failures to use Proximity effectively. While the following chart is not a complete list of classroom situations, it represents problems you may encounter frequently regarding Proximity.

Proximity in Classroom Situations

Classroom Situation	Proximity Failure	Solution
1. Teacher physically leaves room, leaving students unattended.	Non-positioning	Teacher calls for assistance if he or she must leave the room.
2. Teacher sits with back to students while working with individual or group.	Poor Positioning	Teacher repositions to be visible and to be able to see all student activity at all times ("with-it-ness").
3. Teacher fails to look away from textbook or other material.	Lack of Visual Scanning	Teacher looks up frequently to scan all students in classroom.
4. Teacher is at desk not focusing on students as they enter class and resorts to a loud voice to get control.	Combination Poor Positioning Lack of Scanning Lack of Presence	Teacher greets students at door as they enter and reminds them of Expectations for starting work.
5. Teacher is late to class and is unaware of argument brewing between students.	Combination Non-positioning Lack of Scanning	Teacher must be in class before students arrive and must actively scan for potential problems.
6. Students cluster at teacher's desk creating a visual barrier.	Combination Poor Positioning Lack of Scanning	Teacher must either travel to student desks or else manage student consultations one or two at a time *at the side* of teacher's desk.

Consulting for Proximity

While Proximity is only one of the engagement behaviors you will observe and evaluate, the elements of Proximity are mostly physical behaviors performed by the teacher. Those behaviors may impact student behaviors, naturally, and certain student behaviors will help you identify strengths and weaknesses in the teacher's mastery of Proximity skills.

Proximity
Focused Observation Tool

Name: Brain Ust Date: 10/6/09
Grade/Subject: 3rd Observer: T. Jones

Directions: Observing for Physical Positioning, Visual Scanning, and Presence.

✓ = Competent example of Proximity
✓+ = Excellent example of Proximity
✓– = Ineffective attempt of Proximity

The teacher . . .

✓	moves throughout the classroom while instructing (physical positioning)
✓	moves throughout the classroom during independent practice (physical positioning)
✓+	maintains eye contact with students (visual scanning)
✓–	achieves Proximity between small groups (physical positioning)
✓+	communicates authority nonverbally (presence)

Observation Notes:

Keepers:

While moving throughout the classroom, you anticipated problems between Zach and Sally and stopped the action before it started. While calling for attention today, you used purposeful eye contact to draw in nonattending students.

Polishers:

During independent practice, how could you take advantage of Proximity to refocus group A?

Reproducible: Page 167, Appendix

The *Focused Observation Tool* to the left shows a principal's evaluation and observation notes finding a teacher competent in all but one area of physical positioning. Note also that this tool accounts for all three key elements of this skill: Physical Positioning, Visual Scanning, and Presence.

Mr. Jones, the principal, used this completed tool in a debriefing with his teacher and for pointing out the elements of Proximity Mr. Ust performed well. He Identified one element for the teacher to focus on.

Here is another *Focused Observation Tool* for Proximity, this one relating to the Case Study about Rob Selig earlier in this chapter. Notice that the teacher had made marked improvement in Proximity by using visual scanning (eye contact) and by positioning himself by the classroom door to remind students to self-start. In addition, he made nonverbal communication such as physical presence by moving around the room and standing by students who tend to engage in side conversations.

Reminders: To use any *Focused Observation Tool,* plan in advance for a 10– or 15–minute time period that your teacher feels will be advantageous for focusing on that engagement skill. Be sure to tally your teacher's successful uses of the skill on the observation tool.

Be especially keen to find examples that you can justifiably rate

✓+ = Excellent or masterful use of Proximity

and be sure to make note of instances where your teacher could make his or her use of Proximity more effective:

✓– = Attempted but ineffective use of Proximity

Proximity
Focused Observation Tool

Name: Rob Selig Date: 11/1/09
Grade/Subject: 4th Observer: Jim Herb

Directions: Observing for Physical Positioning, Visual Scanning, and Presence.

✓ = Competent example of Proximity
✓+ = Excellent example of Proximity
✓– = Ineffective attempt of Proximity

The teacher . . .

–	moves throughout the classroom while instructing (physical positioning)
✓	moves throughout the classroom during independent practice (physical positioning)
✓&✓–	maintains eye contact with students (visual scanning)
	achieves Proximity between small groups (physical positioning)
✓&✓–	communicates authority nonverbally (presence)

Observation Notes:

Keepers:

Greeted S. at door and reminded them to SS. Used eye-scanning to see S. who self-start. Moved around room giving positive cues to those on task–positioned self by 4 in side conversations and added cueing, and eye contact to stop side-conversations–95% self-started with 85% remaining on task whole SS period.

Polishers:

After you got the attention of students, during mathematics instruction your engagement levels dropped to 45%. How might you transfer what you have learned about proximity and cueing that achieved high levels of engagement during SS to instruction?

Reproducible: Page 167, Appendix

Consulting in Greater Depth for Proximity

Here's another tool for collecting additional or more in-depth data for consulting with teachers about Proximity. This one helps you analyze teacher movements as well as students' related behaviors in the classroom, an approach recommended by such researchers as Carl Glickman (2002) and Sally Zapeda (2007b). Notice that the physical layout of this teacher's classroom (tool pictured) includes six tables, each with three or four students seated, as noted by the evaluator's marks showing on-task behavior by students (the X's) and off-task behavior (–'s.)

Note: You will find additional *Spatial Observation Tools* depicting other classroom layouts in the Appendix (see pp. 170–171.)

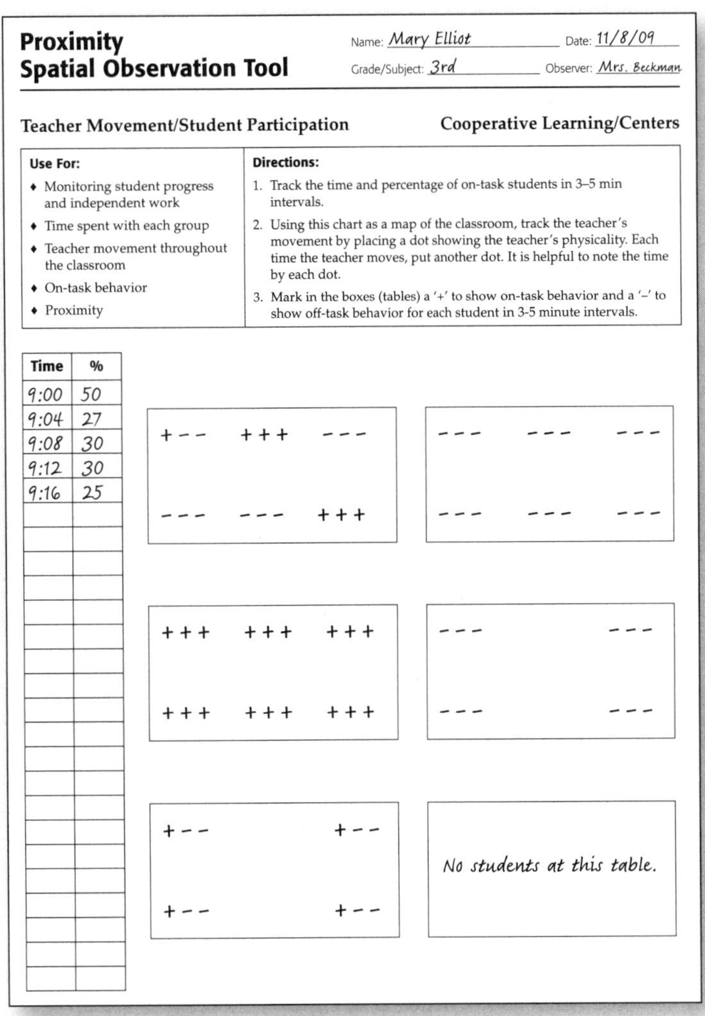

Proximity Spatial Observation Tool

Name: *Mary Elliot* Date: *11/8/09*
Grade/Subject: *3rd* Observer: *Mrs. Beckman*

Teacher Movement/Student Participation **Cooperative Learning/Centers**

Use For:
- Monitoring student progress and independent work
- Time spent with each group
- Teacher movement throughout the classroom
- On-task behavior
- Proximity

Directions:
1. Track the time and percentage of on-task students in 3–5 min intervals.
2. Using this chart as a map of the classroom, track the teacher's movement by placing a dot showing the teacher's physicality. Each time the teacher moves, put another dot. It is helpful to note the time by each dot.
3. Mark in the boxes (tables) a '+' to show on-task behavior and a '–' to show off-task behavior for each student in 3-5 minute intervals.

Time	%
9:00	50
9:04	27
9:08	30
9:12	30
9:16	25

+ – –   + + +   – – –
– – –   – – –   + + +

– – –   – – –   – – –
– – –   – – –   – – –

+ + +   + + +   + + +
+ + +   + + +   + + +

– – –   – – –
– – –   – – –

+ – –   + – –
+ – –   + – –

No students at this table.

Reproducible: Page 168, Appendix

Other Strategies for Consulting about Proximity

To help a teacher gain a better nuanced understanding of Proximity or to help a teacher recognize additional, specific tactics and strategies for employing Proximity in the classroom, consider the following two options:

Option 1: Guide Your Teacher through a Demo Observation

If possible, arrange for your teacher to observe one or two teachers who demonstrate mastery of Proximity in their daily teaching. Have your teacher use a simple *Demo Observation Tool* like the one to the right for this observation in order to (1) identify specific uses of Proximity by the demonstration teacher, (2) enter a brief description of each use of Proximity according to its element: *physical Proximity, visual scanning,* or *presence,* and (3) note the student response for each teacher action. In your debriefing, be sure to ask your teacher not only to identify each use of Proximity by the demonstration teacher, but also to describe the resulting effects of each use of Proximity on student behavior.

Here is an example of a completed tool for observing a demonstration. In this example, Ms. Burke and her administrator have observed Mrs. Collier's 4th grade class.

Proximity Demo Observation Tool

Observer: *Charlotte Burke* Grade/Class: *4th Grade, self-cont.*
Demo Teacher: *Mrs. Helen Collier* Date/Time: *May 20, 2009*

Directions: Describe specific uses of Proximity in three areas (Physical Positioning, Visual Scanning, and Presence), and describe student behavior that results from each use of Proximity.

Physical Positioning Location in the room		**Visual Scanning** Eye-to-eye Contact		**Presence** Posture/Poise	
Teacher Action	**Student Response**	**Teacher Action**	**Student Response**	**Teacher Action**	**Student Response**
Tchr greets students at door reminding of expectations for self-starting.	*All students put materials away and begin work within a minute*	*Teacher winks at two students who are fiddling with "stuff."*	*Put "stuff" in desk and engage in the lesson*	*Teacher smiles as she greets students at door.*	*Smile back at teacher.*
While instructing teacher moves toward two students having a side-conversation.	*Students quit talking and engage in learning.*	*Instructing a small group of students, teacher scans students working at desks, centers.*	*Students working in centers or at desks remain on task*	*Teacher uses an expert voice and stance when doing an attention signal.*	*Students stop what they are doing and attend to the teacher.*

Teacher Transfer: In my classroom, I want to focus on:

1. *Greeting my students at the door every time they enter the classroom and REMINDING them of my expectations for beginning their self-start.*
2. *While instructing, getting my head out of my text so I can know which students are not attending and moving toward them WHILE instructing.*

Reproducible: Page 169, Appendix

Option 2: Shadow Your Teacher for Proximity

Shadowing is a technique for providing real-time guided practice for the teacher with you, intervening as needed to identify opportunities for applying specific Proximity skills.

During your 10– to 15–minute time period with your teacher, stand to one side of the room, crossing behind the teacher as you see fit so that you can offer informational Cues such as *"Anna is not watching"* or *"Group B is not on task,"* and you can offer specific directions like *"Move across the room," "Turn toward Group C more often,"* or *"Stand closer to Zachery."*

As your teacher responds to your guidance, you can switch to using observer Signals from a greater distance like from the back of the room. In advance of a shadowing session, you may identify Signals like these:

Using Observer Signals for Shadowing Proximity

Observer Signal	Indication
Fingers walking.	Move around the classroom.
Point to a location in the room—fingers walk.	Move to a specific location in the room.
Point to your eyes.	Make eye contact with individuals.
Point to your eyes while making a sweeping gesture.	Make eye contact with all students as you scan the classroom.

Coaching for Proximity

As you coach for Proximity, encourage your teacher to think through specific opportunities for using Proximity in the next lesson that you will observe. Ask your teacher to visualize a lesson—in effect, to make mental practice runs—to enhance your teacher's innate understanding and performance of Proximity.

Following are some possible questions that you can use to encourage and assist the teacher in unlocking his or her own thinking about Proximity.

Coaching Conversation for Proximity
Questions for Planning a Visit and Observation

- What is your Proximity goal during your lesson?
- Walk me through your lesson. What opportunities do you see at each step for using physicality and nonverbal Proximity?
- What behavioral problems do you foresee? How can you use Proximity to curtail these possible situations?
- What will you see that will alert you to refocus your Proximity?
- How will you know if your Proximity is successful?

Follow up with your teacher. Encourage a reflective type of conversation to help your teacher cement what he or she did well.

For best results, provide your teacher with your observation data prior to the reflective conversation so the teacher has an opportunity to recognize patterns and to identify questions to discuss. Here are some questions you might use to facilitate this dialogue.

Reflective Conversation Questions
Following the Visit and Observation

- How did it go? Did you meet your goal with Proximity? How do you know?
- Did your plans to address Proximity go as planned? Why or why not?
- What patterns do you see in the data I shared with you?
- What does this data tell you about your uses of Proximity?
- What did you learn about Proximity that you can replicate every time you teach?
- What ONE thing do you want to refine in your use of Proximity skills?

Chapter 7

Cueing

Skill #4

The Big Eight Engagement Skills

EXPECTATIONS
ATTENTION PROMPTS
PROXIMITY
Cueing Teacher uses positive, clear, and effective verbal Cues to clarify, maintain, or redirect activity.
SIGNALS
TIME LIMITS
TASKING
VOICE

7

Cueing

Skill #4

TOOLS for Evaluating CUEING

See Appendix pp. 172–174

Most students want to please their teachers. When students are functioning well and when they receive positive recognition, they are most likely to exhibit good habits and constructive learning practices (Alberto & Troutman, 2006; Cooper, et al., 2007; Ferguson & Houghton, 1992). Most teachers understand the advisability—and the common sense—in recognizing that students need to know what is expected of them—*at all times*—which is what setting Expectations is all about (Chapter 4).

Cueing is a skill closely associated with *Expectations* and functions as a critical support strategy that successful teachers employ regularly and as needed to reinforce Expectations they have set and that students should understand.

Specifically, *Cueing* is verbal recognition offered in a positive way and usually offered publicly for all students to hear. Cueing may be a statement meant for an individual, for a group within a class, or for an entire class. Its purpose is multifold: Cueing clarifies the teacher's Expectations, and it reminds students of what is expected. In addition, since Cueing rewards students for positive results, or simply for exhibiting appropriate behavior, it helps teachers maintain required levels of performance.

Some Cues are strictly behavioral; that is, they intend to correct inappropriate behavior or

CASE STUDY

Dr. Lohrfink began to hear complaints about his new 8th grade special ed teacher:

"Mrs. Solomon doesn't like my child" and "Kids say she is too mean to them."

Upon the principal's first observation in September, he found his teacher began class from her desk. *"Sam, sit down now!"* was her opening direction. Sam shot back, *"I'm just getting the paper you told me to get!"* Dr. Lohrfink perceived tension in the classroom and recognized irritability among many students, not only Sam. Data he entered on his *Time-on-Task Tool* revealed 42% student engagement.

During their debriefing, Mrs. Solomon expressed confidence in her lesson planning, and Dr. Lohrfink agreed, as clearly the teacher had done her planning well. He shared his data with her, pointing out weaknesses in Voice, Tasking, Proximity, and especially Cueing. "Your children seem unhappy. I suspect even the most willing students are reluctant to participate."

Mrs. Solomon confided that her own children have told her that she sees negative things before positive ones. *"I do want*

inattentiveness. These are *social Cues. Academic Cues*, on the other hand, are intended to alert one or more students to Expectations regarding a topic they are working on. And, naturally, some Cues may focus on both social and academic elements at the same time.

At times, Cueing may be a technique a teacher uses to redirect students who are not quite getting it, who are misbehaving, or who simply drift off task for whatever reason. It is important for an evaluator to recognize elements of Cueing because this skill forms a critical communications bridge connecting students' Attention to goals and procedures as well as the Expectations they are required to meet. Cueing is one of several tactics employed by effective teachers to keep communication vital in the classroom and student engagement high.

Keep these points in mind: (1) Cueing should never be a teacher's first-line approach to a problem. (2) Cueing is strictly a reinforcement skill. (3) Cueing does not replace achieving students' Attention, nor does it introduce Expectations or set new ones.

In evaluating a teacher's uses of Cueing, be sure also to note evidence of—or at least be aware of—your teacher's related uses of Attention and Expectation skills.

CASE STUDY – *cont'd*

to be a teacher. . .a good one. I have some ideas. Let me try them."

During the following week when Dr. Lohrfink passed her door, he did not see or hear evidence of change. Hearing *"All of you sit down now and shut up!"* convinced him to work together with this teacher on changing her Cues—her language—to positive statements.

On his next visit, he used a *Focused Observation Tool for Cueing* to write his teacher's statements for them both to analyze later, at which time Mrs. Solomon was quick to spot words she could substitute to make her Cueing statements more positive, more effective.

It worked. On a visit two weeks later, Dr. Lohrfink left a **KEEPER** that pointed out:

> *You are aware of off-task behavior in your room.*
>
> *When you said "Josh, I can see the focus in your eyes!" you made five other children smile at you and focus on the task.*

Purposes of Cueing

Teachers who use Cueing effectively may also be teachers who are adept at communicating clearly. In all likelihood, a teacher who focuses Attention easily and who sets clear Expectations also weaves Cueing statements into classroom dialogue with students. These are examples:

- ✓ *Ely, I had no doubts you would put on your goggles before you lit the burner.*
- ✓ *I can see that Louise already has her journal open and is thinking about the opening scene she is about to write in her autobiography.*
- ✓ *Josh and Henry have their beakers half full, and so do Haley and Alex.*

Teacher moves toward inattentive students and whispers audibly to the attentive ones nearby: *Thank you for focusing on the task.*

A good rule of thumb for Cueing is "Praise two before reminding any." A wise strategy for the teacher is to take the positive approach first ("Praise two. . .") because it gives the off-task child chances to self-correct before receiving a public redirection or redress.

As you observe teachers, look for the positive signposts they offer students—usually as praise for an action occurring at the moment, but also for **clarification** of the teacher's Expectations to reinforce them. **To be effective, a Cue must be directed intentionally and clearly to a specific receiver or set of receivers—one student, two or more students, or to the full class—and the Cue should reference a specific action that the student(s) has taken or should be taking right away.**

Your teacher's Cues should be positive and constructive. A Cue must cite an action done well, and it should be delivered in a tone that is supportive of the student or of the desired outcome. **Since a Cue is a public declaration, it should be delivered so that many or all students hear a message of approval shared not only by its intended recipient(s) but also by the larger group—even the whole class—and is specific enough so that students can replicate the behavior.**

Public discourse between students and teachers—even during those moments when the communication is between just one individual and the teacher—has a significant influence on the classroom learning environment overall. When the discourse is positive, the classroom environment is more conducive to learning. Through discourse, even for the purpose of support or simple **maintenance** of current behavior, a teacher's positive messages strengthen relationships with individual students and with the class as a whole by creating bonds of trust that enable students to feel intellectually and emotionally safe.

One of the greatest benefits of Cueing is the help it offers, directly or indirectly, to those students who are not on task, not focused, or otherwise struggling. Some degree of **redirection** of students is essential for correcting improper or wrong behavior or for getting an individual on task. A good teacher recognizes when a student is off track, or simply misbehaving, and most teachers intervene intuitively and promptly with direction of some kind. Sometimes **redirection** can take gentler, subtler forms, such as when more than one student seems lost or unfocused. For instance, a teacher may point out certain students who are successfully on task, or a teacher may ask on-task students to describe their activity aloud for the class.

As you observe, note the responses of students to the Cues they hear. As you recognize Cueing and note your teacher's positive messages, also note the reactions of (1) the student(s) for whom Cueing was intended and (2) the reactions of other students. For sure, Cueing is successful if one or more students return to task. Cueing is successful if one or more students refocus or adjust activity accordingly. And Cueing can be successful if no more than simple motivation appears to grow (providing, of course, that the Cue was not intended to achieve a more specific change or redirection in behavior.) **In a highly motivated classroom where Cueing may not be necessary to alter outcomes because students are high-functioning, Cueing, nonetheless, helps maintain a positive work environment and keep lines of communication flowing.**

You may find Cueing taking many verbal forms. Good teachers must not only be articulate but must also be creative in their messaging to students, so it would be impossible to catalog and list the many possibilities. However, you can identify at least three main purposes for Cueing, and you may find that most Cueing falls into the following categories, or purposes: Clarification, Maintenance, and Redirection. These are examples of *effective* and *ineffective* Cueing:

Purposes of Cueing

Purpose	Ineffective Cue	Effective Cue
Clarification: To reinforce Expectations	*"At least I see one or two people on the right page. What about the rest of you?"*	*"Excellent, Ellen. You're the first to turn to page 343."*
Maintenance: To recognize what students are doing well	*"Good job, class."*	*"Congratulations, class. You are all at your stations in less than ten seconds. I'm impressed."*
Maintenance: To support or sustain good behavior, correct actions, communication	The teacher thanks Jennifer for being on time but not until the girl is leaving class after dismissal.	After several instances of tardiness, Jennifer has been arriving to class on time. The teacher remarks, *"Jenny, thank you again for making it to class on time, and thank you all. Let's begin together to. . . ."*
Redirection: To correct or alter behavior, practices, or other activity	*"I'm disappointed. Not everybody has switched papers yet."*	*"I see that the members of Groups A and B have switched papers to begin critiquing. Group C, what do you need to do to catch up with them?"*

Recognizing Successful Uses of Cueing

When a teacher makes public statements describing students' specific activities, everybody in class hears the words. Thus, by incorporating Expectations of students into the language of complimentary statements, a teacher simultaneously reinforces the positive aspects of student activity or behavior while clarifying goals or other information for all. In short, the teacher moves students forward with approval and clarification while reinforcing and encouraging them. The research is clear: Students meet Expectations when goals are clear and reinforced. Generally, social as well as academic behaviors tend to improve in classroom environments where teachers apply praise that supports Expectations (Winne and Butler, 1994; Yawkey, 1971).

Discussions with your teacher about Cueing must address the Expectations that underlie or precede the Cues. For instance, to discuss a classroom event in which your teacher needed to re-direct a student, be sure to discuss the specific Expectations that had been set beforehand.

The following are examples of Cueing applied after teachers have set Expectations. In some cases, teachers have set Expectations in previous class sessions.

Example 1: 7th Grade Group Work

Mrs. Smart is working with three students in a group at the front of her room while other students work at centers. She notices that one group at the science reference center has completed its work and has moved on. *"Thank you, Sally and Patty and Mikhaila, for leaving the science center in order for the next group."* She scans the class. *"Sean and Andy, you can move on to science if you're ready."* The boys move promptly to the center that the girls have left. (In follow-up discussion with her principal, Mrs. Smart recognizes that her Cue to the girls was a form of **maintenance**—a direct reference to the Expectation she had set earlier in the week. She also recognizes that her direction to the boys was for **clarification,** a reminder of those same Expectations. The clarification would have been **redirection**, Mrs. Smart concludes, had the boys not been prepared to move on to the science center. Ideally, she and her principal also conclude, the boys should have been more alert to Expectations and should have noticed that the science center was available and would not have needed clarification.

Example 2: 2nd Grade Base-Ten Lesson

Mr. Jones is preparing to introduce base-ten. Before distributing materials for a hands-on lesson, he uses an Attention Prompt: *"Class, be ready in five. . .I see Brock has his eyes on me. Good. . .Sally, thank you for having your area cleaned and ready."* Mr. Jones then sets Expectations for using the blocks: *"During our lesson today, each group will have a bucket of blocks. You will be given numbers to show using the blocks. As soon as I give you the number, you will have five seconds to start your work. When you have finished arranging the number, stand up, and I will know you are ready for me to check your work."* Mr. Jones hands a number on a flash card to each table and uses Cues to countdown toward starting work: *"Five. . .Group A has their blocks out. Four. . .Group C. . .great job sharing the work within the group. Three. . .Group D, Wow! You are really thinking together. Two. . .One. Group B, you're the first to stand. Excellent."*

Example 3: 1st Grade Centers

It is time for lunch in Mrs. Samuel's classroom. As students work in centers, Mrs. Samuel moves in quick succession to each group and whispers Expectations: *"Keep working until you hear the bell. I will be looking for the students who are putting away their center quickly and quietly."* And then to the whole class: *"I will know you are ready to go to lunch when your area is cleaned and you are sitting quietly at your desk."* The bell rings, students begin rapidly cleaning up except for Zach and Andy who throw crayons at each other. As she moves toward the two boys, Mrs. Samuel Cues: *"Writing center, thank you for working together so well. Dramatic center, excellent! You even hung up the costumes neatly."* Arriving at the boys' table, Mrs. Samuel whispers to them, *"Boys, please see me before you go to lunch recess."* During recess, Mrs. Samuel has Zach and Andy practice cleaning up.

Recognizing Opportunities for Using Cueing

Even effective teachers sometimes miss opportunities for using Cueing. Be on the lookout for opportunities to employ this strategy, especially for purposes like **clarification** and **redirection**, as these two often are necessary for getting children on track to learn. The following chart offers a few more examples, showing how ineffective Cues or missed opportunities can be overcome:

Opportunities for Improving Cueing		
Classroom Situation	**Cueing Failure**	**Solution**
1. All but four students begin independent work following their teacher's instructions. Two giggle to each other; one is drawing; one appears asleep.	*"Boys, cut it out!"* *"Eddie, put that away. Now!"* *"Wake up, Lizzie. You're not home in bed."*	Teacher moves closer to the four students, makes eye contact and **redirects** aloud, *"We're almost all on task. Boys, it will be good to have you aboard. You, too, Lizzie."* Then, as they comply, *"Thanks. Let's all get started."*
2. Students know they begin every class by writing the answer to a "bell ringer" question on the board. Paul and Ed are pushing each other as others begin to write.	The teacher ignores the two boys.	The teacher stands closer to the boys and asks them quietly to begin or else to separate. Then, with approval aloud, *"Excellent, Paul and Ed. I'm looking forward to reading your answer."*
3. The recess bell rings. Students line up to enter class. Two students linger on the playground.	The teacher calls out, *"Boys, line up NOW. Do you know how sick I am of waiting for you to line up?"*	Teacher first acknowledges the 21 students on line: *"I'm proud of you for lining up so quickly."* Then, after asking students on line to ask each other what they enjoyed most about recess, the teacher moves closer to the tarrying boys. *"Boys, next recess you and I will practice lining up so we don't hold up the class."*
4. Most study while two girls chat behind their open books.	From her desk, the teacher calls out, *"Girls, quit talking. You're disturbing everyone."*	The teacher moves toward the girls' desks while saying, *"Very good. Sally is deep into her book. Tom, you look engrossed."* The two girls see the teacher approach and resume reading. *"Thank you for refocusing," the teacher whispers.*

Consulting for Cueing

With your teacher, discuss **Cueing** as a form of positive reminding, a verbal technique for encouraging appropriate behaviors in order to reinforce Expectations. If necessary, discuss the possible impact on students of making changes to the tone of communication. Encourage your teacher to remember to "Praise two (two positive Cues) before reminding any," meaning that at least two positive observations should precede any reminder. **Positive Cues, or messages, have positive impacts on classroom tone and on learning in general.**

Cueing
Focused Observation Tool

Name: *Mr. Parsons* Date: *11/5/09*
Grade/Subject: *6th math* Observer: *E. Williams*

Directions: Use the rating scale to rate performance for both Parts A and B

✓ = Apparent or competent use of Cueing during an evaluation interval
✓+ = Excellent or masterful use of Cueing during an evaluation interval
✓– = Attempted but ineffective use of Cueing during interval
NA or simply leaving an entry blank indicates "not applicable"

Part A: Uses of Cueing. Apply the rating scale to overall performance

	Teacher offers two positive Cues before reminding students of Expectations
✓+	Teacher offers Cues that are clear and understandable
✓	Teacher uses Cueing with other skills such as Proximity or Signals
✓+	Teacher offers Cues for clarification of Expectations
✓+	Teacher offers Cues for maintenance of social or academic Expectations
✓–	Teacher uses Cueing for redirection of students as needed

Part B: Verbatim Uses of Cueing. Use the spaces below to record specific verbal Cues and to rate the effectiveness of each

Verbatims:	**Rating**
"I appreciate how table 5 starting working immediately!"	✓+
"Put that away right now!"	✓–
"I like how Sam is focusing on correct spelling."	✓+
"WOW Samantha, thank you for sharing without being asked!"	✓+
"Quinten, stop that now!"	✓–

Observation Notes:

Keepers:
Your specific cues for maintenance and clarification of Expectations were excellent. Your Cues matched your Expectations. Students responded to your positive Cues.

Polishers:
How can you remind yourself to use two positive cues before reprimanding individual students?

Reproducible: Page 172, Appendix

The *Focused Observation Tool* on the left shows one principal's evaluation and observation notes in which she rates Mr. Parsons competent in all areas but using Cueing for redirection. Accordingly, the principal suggests under *Polishers* that Mr. Parsons use two positive Cues before reprimanding individual students.

Note also that this tool accounts for the three key purposes of this skill: clarification, maintenance, and redirection. In the example, the principal points to one *Polisher* so that the teacher has a goal of developing specific behavioral Cues rather than using only general statements of praise. If a teacher feels unsure about constructing specific Cues, you might suggest using a *Looks Like/Sounds Like* chart (see Expectations, pp. 36 or 41.)

Reminders for Consulting about Cueing

1. Schedule a preliminary visit of 10 to 15 minutes to focus specifically on Cueing.
2. Use a *Focused Observation Tool* to rate specific skills relating to Cueing. For instance:

   ✓+ = Excellent or masterful use of Cueing.

   ✓– = Attempted but ineffective use of Cueing.

3. Leave behind the completed tool, or a copy, showing *Keepers* and *Polishers* so your teacher can consider these for your subsequent debriefing.
4. Make note of one or two *Polishers*, specific Cues or Cueing techniques that your teacher needs to improve.
5. Always phrase *Polishers* in question form.

Consulting in Greater Depth for Cueing

For more in-depth data, you might use a *Depth Observation Tool*. The model below will remind you that the Cueing statements you hear during an observation might be positive (e.g., for clarification, maintenance, redirection), or they may be neutral; that is, they may be offered simply to introduce directions or to ask questions. Such Cues are perfectly fine. Other statements may be negative (simple scolding is one example). Negative statements often are simply just that: negative, perhaps even counterproductive.

In this completed model, an evaluator has returned to his teacher's classroom specifically to collect a variety of the teacher's verbatim statements for a follow-up consultation about verbal interactions with students. Using this *Depth-Consultation Tool* for Cueing, the evaluator attempts to collect specific examples of Cueing as well as examples of other frequently offered statements. He collects a range of statements for a full and focused discussion with the teacher about successful—and less-than-successful—examples of Cueing.

Notice that the columns for entering verbatims into this tool are arranged from left to right according to tone: ***positive—neutral—negative***. This column format may help you demonstrate and assist

Cueing Depth Observation Tool

Observer: *Nathan Smeldwig* Grade/Class: *7th-B*
Demo Teacher: *Yanni Donavich* Date/Time: *10/18/09*

Skill Definition: A Cue is a positive verbal reinforcement to assist one or more students to meet social or academic Expectations
Directions: During a 15–minute observation, record statements verbatim into the categories where they seem to fit. Notice that columns for Cueing (on the left) are positive; other kinds of statements may be neutral in tone (middle.) Place negative Cues such as scolding in the right column

Representative Statements Including Cueing

Cueing Statements (Positive)				Information, Directions, Questions (Neutral)	Scolding (Negative)
Clarification	Approval	Maintenance	Redirection		
hank you, Ellen, for having your eyes on me, I can tell you are ready to learn.		*Students, may I have your attention, now (pausing with eye contact).*	*During centers today, I will be looking for students who know exactly where to go next.*	*Open your math books to page 24.*	*Samuel, sit down.*
Table 3, I love how your materials are all put away and you are standing quietly with your chairs tucked in.		*I admire how this class begins working immediately! Thank you!*	*Rachel, I watched you put your materials away and move immediately to join your partner.*	*Today we will be learning how to add fractions with common denominators.*	*Bob, do you know where your seat is?*
				We will be transitioning into study partners in two minutes.	*Jose, you didn't bother bringing your homework back, again.*
					BOB (yelled from reading group)! Get busy NOW!

Tally/Frequency: Kinds of Statements

Kind of Statement	Apparent Frequency (Tally)
Clarification Cue	*III*
Maintenance Cue	*II*
Redirection Cue	*III*
Neutral Information	*IIIII IIIII*
Negative/Scolding, Sarcasm, etc.	*IIIII*

Reproducible: Page 173, Appendix

your teacher in setting a goal to move statements out of the scolding/sarcasm (negative) column by increasing the frequency of constructing positive Cues for the information.

If you keep track or tally the frequency of different kinds of Cueing statements, you can use this data to illustrate for your teacher the kinds and frequencies of statements he or she is using to communicate. Such information will assist in setting a goal to avoid statements like those in the scolding/sarcasm (negative) column by moving towards the kinds of Cueing information in the columns that represent positive and neutral support.

Other Strategies for Consulting about Cueing

To work further on Cueing, you might consider the following three optional strategies:

Option 1: Guide Your Teacher through a Demo Observation.

Cueing Demo Observation Tool

Observer: *Jack Cage* Grade/Class: *2nd, self-contained*

Demo Teacher: *Amanda Jones* Date/Time: *09/25/09*

Skill Definitions: A Cue is a positive verbal reinforcement for any of these purposes:

Clarification of Expectations **Maintenance** of expected behavior or activity

Redirection toward correct behavior or activity

Directions: Write examples of your demonstration teacher's Cues in the column labeled "Teacher Action" for the appropriate kind of Cue. For each Cue you enter, describe the "Student Response" in the column to its right

Clarification of Expectations		Maintenance of Expectations		Redirection to Correct Activity	
Teacher Action	Student Response	Teacher Action	Student Response	Teacher Action	Student Response
Teacher gives Expectations for a transition "Move quickly and quietly to your location. I will know you are ready when your eyes ore on me."	*Most students rapidly transition following the teacher's Expectations.*	*After several days of practicing beginning a task within five seconds, the teacher remarked, "Tables 1 and 2 remembered to start within 5 seconds today!"* *During the transition, the teacher says, "Joycelynn is moving quietly." "Sam has his eyes on me"*	*Two other tables immediately began working on the self-start.* *For tables that are slow to transition, reinforce Expectations with Cueing reminders.*	*While using Proximity between small groups, teacher states, "Table 1 has their materials out, pencils ready, and are flat on their chairs."* *This statement was said while standing by an off-task group.*	*Table 1 continues working. Table 3 begins focusing.*

Teacher Transfer: In my classroom, I want to focus on:

Clarification: Use praise that matches the Expectations I have set. If I use the same verbiage, then I will be reinforcing my Expectations.

Reproducible: Page 174, Appendix

If possible, arrange for your teacher to observe one or two teachers who demonstrate mastery of Cueing in their daily teaching. During this observation, have your teacher use a simple tool like the *Demo Observation Tool* on the left in order to (1) identify specific uses of Cueing by the demonstration teacher, (2) enter a brief description of each use of Cueing according to its purpose: *clarification, maintenance, redirection,* and (3) note the student response for each teacher action. In your de-briefing with your teacher, be sure to ask him or her not only to identify key uses of Cueing by the demonstration teacher, but also to describe the resulting effects of each of those uses upon students and upon overall classroom environment and tone. In addition, help your teacher set goals.

Option 2: Shadow Your Teacher for Cueing

Shadowing allows you or another observer to intervene as needed to identify opportunities for applying specific Cueing skills. For instance, you might offer social Cues such as *"Michael is not listening"* or *"The two girls at the rear table are whispering,"* or academic Cues such as *"Alex hasn't found the right page yet"* or *"Several students seem puzzled about the term 'sublimation.'"*

Here is a transcript of an actual demonstration event—a Tale of Shadow Cueing:

Bob Jones, elementary school administrator, has worked on Cueing with Samantha Tucker, third grade teacher, for two weeks after receiving complaints from parents about Samantha's "negative approach." In two observations, Bob gave his teacher specific data showing a lack of positive Cueing. Her negatives outnumber her positives 10 to 1

Bob's advice to work on Cueing leaves Samantha unclear about when to use Cueing, nor does she believe a Cueing statement will work as well as simply telling *a child not to do something.*

Bob determines that Samantha is struggling because she doesn't know precisely when to utilize Cueing, so he offers to shadow to help her see the actual benefits of Cueing and to begin internalizing the skill.

Bob and Samantha chose a 10–minute time interval during a direct instruction lesson for their first try at shadowing. Bob began by directing*—telling Samantha exactly what to say—so he stood strategically at the left side of the room. As Samantha gave her Attention Prompt for the lesson, Bob walked behind her and whispered, "Say, 'Table 3, thank you for having your materials ready so quickly!'" Samantha made the statement aloud, looked around the room, and then felt pleased as other tables quickly got their materials ready.*

As Samantha began her lesson on word work, Bob noticed that Ben and another boy seemed to be daydreaming, so Bob moved behind Samantha to say,"Tell John and Sean you know they really do understand this and thank them for focusing." Samantha did so and noticed both boys back on task.

Once all children were working independently, Bob asked Samantha what she saw happen when she utilized the Cues. Samantha was encouraged by the results, so Bob scheduled yet another Cueing shadow session for the next day when Bob moved to guiding*—asking Samantha a question to guide her rather than giving her verbatim Cues. This time, when Samantha gave the Attention Prompt, Bob walked behind her and said, "Cue to clarify your Expectations" so Samantha said, "WOW! Table 5 was ready in 3 seconds!" which encouraged table 1 to get ready.*

During this lesson, Bob whispered to Samantha, "Ben is off task again. Notice what Sally is doing. Use a redirectional Cue." In response, Samantha moved toward the children and said, "Sally, thank you for having your attention on the white board. You are SUCH a good learner!" Ben immediately refocused his attention.

With children working independently, Bob and Samantha then discussed the positive changes in classroom environment due to Cueing. Samantha felt ready to work on Cueing as she began to see its benefits so she used a reminder technique when her principal is not there to shadow her—she placed a piece of masking tape around her wrist so she could place a tally mark every time she used a Cue. Her goal, she told Bob, was to mark at least ten Cues before lunch!

Bob decided to continue to gradually release Samantha and talked to her before school on the day of the next scheduled shadowing. They decided that when Samantha would need to use a clarifying or maintenance Cue, Bob would give her a thumbs-up Signal from the back of the room. When Samantha would need to use a Cue to redirect behavior, Bob would point towards the offending student with one hand and give a thumbs-up with the other. This session lasted 10 minutes, during which Samantha gave four Cues without any signals from Bob. As her lesson intensified, Bob Cued Samantha for redirection.

During this visit, Bob filled out a Focused Observation Tool for Cueing so Samantha could see the positive results of her Cueing. Samantha and Bob debriefed, and Bob shared his positive information (see tool on preceding page) *and Samantha shared her tape. She had given 15 Cues the previous afternoon!*

Option 3: Reflective Counting

Have your teacher put a piece of masking tape around a wrist. Each time the teacher uses a positive Cue, the teacher tallies a mark on the tape. The teacher can then work toward increasing the number of positive Cues (see preceding anecdote.)

Coaching for Cueing

Once your teacher begins to understand Cueing, move to a coaching stance to increase your teacher's ability to self-direct. Help your teacher think through occasions that might require Cueing, how effective the Cueing has been, and what refinements to make to future Cues.

Following are some possible questions that you can use to encourage and assist your teacher in unlocking his or her own thinking about Cueing.

Coaching Conversation for Cueing
Questions for Planning a Visit and Observation

- What is your Cueing goal during your lesson?
- What Expectations will you give your students? What Cues will you use to reinforce your Expectations?
- Which student(s) will be unfocused during your lesson? What behaviors do these students exhibit that are problematic? How can you use strategic Cueing to curtail these possible situations?
- How will you know if your Cueing is successful?

Here are some questions you might use to facilitate a reflective dialogue that considers data you collected prior to this conversation:

Reflective Conversation Questions
Following the Visit and Observation

- How did it go? Did you meet your goal with Cueing? How do you know?
- Did your plans to address Cueing go as planned? Why or why not?
- What patterns do you see in the data I shared with you?
- What does this data tell you about your uses of Cueing? How does this affect the overall environment in your classroom?
- What did you learn about Cueing that you want to replicate every time you teach?
- What ONE thing do you want to refine further about your Cueing skills?

Chapter 8

Signals

Skill #5

The Big Eight Engagement Skills

EXPECTATIONS
ATTENTION PROMPTS
PROXIMITY
CUEING
Signals Teacher employs Signals to give students ways of showing kinesthetically when they have completed a short task and are ready for the next step.
TIME LIMITS
TASKING
VOICE

8

Signals

Skill #5

TOOLS for Evaluating SIGNALS

See Appendix pages. 175–177

CASE STUDY

Jose Sanchez, a new 2nd grade teacher, was ready to call it quits only six weeks into the school year. His greatest frustrations, he reported to his principal, were unresponsive, disengaged students in his classroom.

Preliminary observation data showed average student engagement of 25% in Jose's room, and it was not consistent. At times, engagement spiked to 85% and at other times dropped to zero. Jose achieved high student engagement when he used Attention Prompts, but 5 minutes into direct instruction, students became bored, disinterested, disengaged. Subsequent observation data made apparent that Jose seemed to expect his 2nd graders to sit focused through lectures that were way too long. A chasm had grown between teacher and students.

In a debriefing after two *Time-on-Task* observations, Jose and his principal discussed adding Signals into instruction. The principal explained Signaling and gave Jose examples to show how to use a kinesthetic Signal and added, *"Jose, you have told me you tend to answer your own questions because your students are not responding. Try asking them to write their answers in the*

Effective teachers use **Signals** to guide students actively through the learning process (Carnine, et al., 2004; Godfrey, et al., 2003; Greenwood, et al., 2002; Sutherland, et al., 2003). **Using *Signals*, teachers give students ways to kinesthetically show when they have completed a short task and are ready for the next step.** For instance, your teacher might say *"Open your book to page 5 and Signal me you're ready by putting your finger on the first word."*

A common problem for struggling teachers is their temptation to give directions without providing students a way to Signal that they are ready to move on to the next phase, whatever that may be. When students don't know specifically what to do—even for a few seconds!—they find something else, and it is rarely something the teacher would have chosen for them.

Children have an innate desire to please and to respond as their teacher would like them to. A problem occurs when students are left without a way to Signal their teacher that they are ready to respond, begin the lesson, transition, etc. It is then that a cyclical problem occurs: For instance, a teacher asks students to get out their math books; some students immediately do this and others lag, so the teacher repeats in frustration, *"Get your math books out." "Get your math books out."* Since most children like to Signal adults, a more effective Signal in this situation might be *"Hold up your math book so I can see the cover."*

Each teacher has the power and obligation to use Signaling as an interactive means of communicating clearly and effectively. An evaluator should recognize elements of Signaling because a teacher's lack of this skill may contribute to instructional and management ineffectiveness—and to confusion in the classroom. It stands to reason that a teacher's effective use of Signaling should be a critical focus for your observations and for a teacher's ongoing development, particularly if your teacher struggles with off-task behavior.

Elements of Signals

Signals, simply put, are physical indicators *from students* to indicate that they have understood, that they are ready, or that they are in the right physical or mental location for proceeding with a task. Unlike Cues (Chapter 7), which are verbal indicators that come directly from the teacher, Signals come from students. Signals are simple demonstrations by children that they are in step with their teacher's Expectations.

Teachers who use Signals may have well-paced classrooms because their students don't lose time by not knowing what to do or by unnecessary disruptions.

When you observe primary classrooms, you may expect to see rudimentary Signals that young children can use easily, such as a thumbs-up sign, a pencil held up, a hand raised to show readiness. In middle and high school classrooms, you may expect to see more contextual versions of Signals encouraged by a teacher. For instance, students in a science lab might hold goggles in the air to indicate they have located a key piece of safety equipment. Or 9th grade students locating line 4 in Act I of *Romeo and Juliet* can hold up four fingers to indicate they are ready to discuss its significance.

Whichever grade level you observe, be alert to communication from child to teacher indicating readiness. Chances are, your teacher will

CASE STUDY – *cont'd*

air. In that way students will have a concrete, simple Signal for responding to you."

Jose tried using Signals the very next day and asked his principal to observe while he guided his students through a practice sheet. Later, data on the principal's *Depth Observation Tool* revealed that students did the problems but then veered off task. More, Bob did not appear to know who had finished and who hadn't. Students had not been given ways to Signal their teacher at key points.

This poor result led to a good outcome, however, because it convinced Jose to think of some new Signals for students to try:

1. put your pencil in the air,
2. lay your pencil on top of desk,
3. whisper-check your answer with your neighbor, and
4. hold up your paper when you are finished.

When he incorporated the Signals into his various routines, Jose began to get results—students used the Signals, students connected more directly with Jose, students appeared livelier—and the teacher began to see that students who had been unresponsive now became noticeably more engaged.

Jose made a practice of having students Signal him when they (1) had books out, (2) were finished with a problem, (3) thought of or knew an answer, and (4) put things away and were ready for recess.

By mid-year, Jose felt he had made progress with student engagement. His principal agreed. As the teacher moved forward honing other engagement skills, he kept in mind an important insight about Signals: If he failed to expect students to Signal, they would find something else to do—off task! ♦♦♦

prompt the Signal, having already developed this procedure—this Expectation—from the beginning of the year. Identify the aspects of your teacher's use of Signals that you think speak the loudest to students. Be on the lookout for Signals from students that indicate they readily comprehend or follow their teacher. Recognize when Expectations aren't being met because students have not been prepared to Signal readiness. In short, you will look for your teacher's direction in relation to students' method of response so you can identify effective Signals from ineffective ones:

Identifying Effective and Ineffective Signals	
Ineffective Signals	**Effective Signals**
Teacher directs students to open math books to page 10, repeating the direction several times as some students have responded and have now found something else to do while waiting.	Teacher says, "*Open your math book to page 10. Give me a thumbs-up when you are ready.*"
During a spelling test, the teacher speaks a word and then waits for students to be ready. When she speaks the next word, some are not focused and soon are asking, "*What was the word?*"	During a spelling test, the teacher dictates the word and directs students, "*As soon as you are finished, write the word as many times in the air as you can before I stay, STOP!*"

We know that pacing problems frequently result when a lesson is too slow, when not enough material is being taught, or when students feel bored. Pacing problems also can occur when students have not been encouraged to connect—in short, they have not been directed to Signal.

Recognizing Successful Uses of Signals

Teachers who use Signals consciously provide a method for students to kinesthetically respond with each direction. Here is an example:

Example: 2nd Grade Math Lesson

During her lesson on fractions, Mrs. Smith begins with direct instruction. She transitions students to the rug and instructs, "*Signal when you are ready to learn about fractions by drawing a half-circle in the air.*" Students respond so Mrs. Smith can see which students do not understand what a half-circle is. Next she shows students a circle and tells them it is a complete pie. She tells students to pretend that they can have ½ of the pie or ¼ of the pie. She has students Signal by standing "*if you would like ½ of the* pie" and kneeling "*if you would like ¼ of the pie.*" She repeats this Signaling procedure with a square and a rectangle. Students transition to their tables. Mrs. Smith instructs students to Signal that they *"are ready for your next task by whispering to your partner if you would rather have ½ a pie or ¼ of a pie."* Then, for guided practice, Mrs. Smith hands white boards to students and gives the students a fraction. She tells students to draw the fraction on their white boards. When they are ready, students are to *"Signal by putting your pen down on your white board."* After several problems, students are ready for independent practice, so Mrs. Smith instructs them to *"Signal when you have finished the first five problems by raising your hands."*

Recognizing Missed Opportunities for Signals

While the following is by no means a complete list of Signal failures, it charts some of the most frequent problems you may encounter as you observe for Signals.

Signals in Classroom Situations		
Classroom Situation	**Signal Failure**	**Solution**
1. Time is wasted when teacher directs students to take out their math books.	Students are not given a Signal to show that they are ready.	Teacher tells students to give thumbs-up when their book is out.
2. A class misses its turn to go to lunch because students take too long to line up for lunch.	Students are not given clear Expectations or a Signal to show they are ready.	Teacher gives a behavioral Expectation. *"Please line up for lunch quietly." "Whisper to your neighbor what you will be doing at recess when you are ready."*
3. Chaos ensues when students read chorally or chant vocabulary words.	Teacher has not given students an Expectation or a clear Signal to help them start together.	Teacher gives students both a Signal and a behavioral Expectation, such as *"When I snap my finger, begin choral reading of the sentence I'm pointing to in our book."* [Then teacher snaps fingers to begin.]
4. Many students shout their answers at once when teacher asks a question.	Teacher hasn't taught students an Expectation or a way to Signal that they have an answer to a question.	Before asking a question, teacher gives the Expectation and a Signal: *"Place your finger on your chin when you have the answer to this question."*

Consulting for Signals

Expect to observe and look for Signals among other engagement skills. Elements of Signals are kinesthetic behaviors performed by students as directed by the teacher. These behaviors may impact pacing. Noting student behaviors will help you identify strengths and weaknesses in your teacher's mastery of this skill.

Signals Focused Observation Tool

Name: *Sue Riding* Date: *11/1/09*
Grade/Subject: *2nd math lesson* Observer: *J. Smith*

Skill Definition: Signals are kinesthetic or other nonverbal indicators from students showing that they understand or are ready for a task.

Directions: Observe for clear directions (Expectations) that include physical indicators (Signals) from children. Use the following rating system:

- ✓ = Strategy is apparent
- ✓+ = Strategy is well done
- ✓– = Strategy is attempted but weak

The teacher . . .

	establishes behavioral Expectations that include a kinesthetic method of response from students
✓	has students use Signals to verify that they are ready for a task to begin (i.e. put your finger on the first word on the page)
✓✓	has students use Signals to engage in direct instruction (e.g., raise your hand if…count on your fingers how many ideas you have. . .)

Observation Notes:

Keepers:

Students responded to signals during your lesson. The use of thumbs-up, writing in the air, whispering to neighbors kept the pacing rapid, kept students engaged, and provided you with assessment opportunities.

Polishers:

During your transition, how could students signal you that they are ready once they have reached the rug?

Reproducible: Page 175, Appendix

In this model *Focused Observation Tool* for Signals, the principal's observation notes find Sue Riding competent in all but one area of providing a clear direction and following up with a kinesthetic method for students to communicate that they are ready. Note that this tool lists and identifies the key elements of Signaling to help direct your observation and data collection.

The completed tool can be used in debriefing to point out elements of Signaling performed well plus one element to focus on. In this case, the principal notes only one *Polisher*, to improve transitions by having students Signal that they are ready once they have completed the transition to the rug. The specific goal gives Sue a specific, do-able, and deliberate focus for moving forward.

Consulting In Greater Depth for Signals

A *Depth Observation Tool* for Signals is another vehicle for collecting additional or more in-depth data. The next model analyzes teacher directions as well as students' kinesthetic responses. Note that Ms. Rivers has mastered Signals and might now be an excellent choice for demonstration teacher.

In addition, her principle suggests that Jody consider another engagement skill to focus on and hone.

Signals
Depth Observation Tool

Name: Jody Rivers Date: 11/4/09
Grade/Subject: 3rd Literacy Observer: Tyson Verhaal

Directions: 1. Write the teacher direction and students' responses or Signal
2. Write the percentage of students that respond appropriately

Teacher Direction	Kinesthetic Response	%
I am going to ask you some questions about fractions. Give me a thumbs-up if you know the answer to each question: what is ½ plus ½? What is ¼ plus ¼?	Students are focused. Most are responding with thumbs in the air, some have thumbs-down, some have thumbs sideways (kind of know).	95
Open your book to page 27. Point to a word that starts with the same letter as your name when you are ready.	Students point to the word. Two students are trying to find their books.	90
When you finish problem #1, write your answer in the air as many times as you can before I say stop!	Students rapidly do the problem and write in the air.	85
Try problem #2. Whisper your answer to your neighbor when you are finished. If you are stuck, put your pencil in the air.	85% of the students rapidly begin working. A few are unfocused, uncertain as to how to solve the problem.	85 90
Take out your white boards. I will give you a problem Solve it on your white board. Hold it up when you are finished.	Students do the problems as they are given on their white boards and hold them up.	100

Observation Notes:

Keepers:

Excellent! Your signals kept your students very actively engaged! They knew exactly what to do! May I bring other teachers to observe you?

Polishers:

Think about the next engagement skill you'd like to focus on.

Reproducible: Page 176, Appendix

Other Strategies for Consulting about Signaling

To help sharpen your teacher's understanding of Signaling or to help a teacher recognize tactics and strategies for employing Signals in the classroom, you might consider the following strategies:

Signals Demo Observation Tool

Observer: *April Delacruz* Grade/Class: *3rd Grade, self-cont.*
Demo Teacher: *Mr. Don Trujillo* Date/Time: *10/25/09 11:00am*

Directions: Identify specific uses of Signaling by students that result from the demonstration teacher's direction or Expectation. Then describe students' responses (the Signals they give).

Teacher Direction	Kinesthetic or Nonverbal Response
Take out your paper and pencil and put your name on top of your paper. Write your name in the air when you are ready	*Most students are writing in the air after 30 seconds, but two students can't find their pencils.*
Open your novel to the page you have bookmarked. Whisper to your neighbor what last happened your book.	*All students but two have books open and are whispering. The two appear confused.*
It is time for recess. Quietly put your books away and put your coat on. Stand behind your desk when you are ready.	*Within 1 minute all students are standing with their coats on.*

Teacher Transfer: In my classroom, I want to set and refine this Expectation:
1. *Transitions: Give students a direction that includes behavioral expectations.*
2. *Response: For EVERY direction that I give students, provide a kinesthetic method for response.*

Reproducible: Page 177, Appendix

Guide Your Teacher through a Demo Observation. If possible, arrange for your teacher to observe one or two teachers who demonstrate mastery of Signaling in their daily teaching. Have your teacher use a simple tool for this observation in order to (1) look for specific uses of Signaling by the demonstration teacher, (2) enter a brief description of Signaling as it is demonstrated by *Teacher Direction*, and (3) note the *Student [Kinesthetic] Response* for each teacher action. In your debriefing, ask your teacher to identify each use of Signaling by the demonstration teacher and to describe the resulting effects of each use of Signaling upon student behavior. In addition, help set goals for whichever elements of Signaling your teacher wishes to transfer into the classroom.

To the left is an example of a completed tool for observing a demonstration teacher. In this example, Ms. Delacruz and her administrator have observed Mr. Trujillo's 3rd grade class.

Shadow Your Teacher for Signals: Shadowing is a way you can provide real-time guided practice for your teacher. Schedule a 10– to 15–minute time period. Stand to one side of the room, crossing behind the teacher as you see fit so that you can offer Cues to your teacher. Use any of the following methods while shadow-coaching: Directing, Guiding, and Signaling:

Shadow Coaching for Signals	
Method	**Examples**
Directing	Say, *"Open your book to page ____. Point to the first word."* Say, *"Move to the rug. Fold your arms and sit up straight as soon as you get there."* Say, *"Look up if you're ready. Smile if you're ready. Clap hands if you're ready."*
Guiding	*"How could students signal you they're ready?"* *"Look at ____________. Give a signal."*
Signaling	Make an S in the air. (Give a signal).

Coaching for Signaling

To coach for Signaling, assist your teacher mentally rehearse opportunities that may present themselves for using Signals in an upcoming lesson. Consider using these questions:

Coaching Conversation for Signals
Questions for Planning a Visit and Observation

- What is your Signaling goal during your lesson?
- Walk me through your lesson. What transitions will there be? What directions will you give at each transition? How will you have students kinesthetically respond?
- During the direct instruction portion of your lesson, what opportunities for Signals are there?
- During guided practice, what opportunities for Signals are there?
- During independent practice, how will students Signal that they need help or are ready to be checked off?
- What behavioral problems do you foresee? How can you use Signals to curtail these possible situations?
- What will you see that will alert you to use a Signal?
- How will you know if your Signaling is successful?

Here are some questions you might use to facilitate a dialogue to celebrate strengths and to identify one element to consciously address in moving forward to refine Signaling skills. Consider providing your teacher with your observation data prior to this conversation:

Reflective Conversation Questions Following the Visit and Observation

- To what degree did you meet your goal with Signaling? How do you know?
- Did your plans to use Signals go as planned? Why or why not?
- What patterns do you see in the data I shared with you?
- What does this data tell you about your uses of Signals?
- What did you learn about Signals that you want to replicate when you teach?
- What ONE thing do you want to refine further about your Signal skills?

Chapter 9

Time Limits

Skill #6

The Big Eight Engagement Skills

EXPECTATIONS
ATTENTION PROMPTS
PROXIMITY
CUEING
SIGNALS
Time Limits Teacher identifies and communicates specific times for beginning and completing tasks.
TASKING
VOICE

9

Time Limits

Skill #6

TOOLS for Evaluating TIME LIMITS

See Appendix pages. 178–181

CASE STUDY

Jess White was stunned when he saw the data his principal had collected during a 30-minute *Time-On-Task* observation of his 3rd grade class during literacy block, showing that 10 of the 30 minutes were wasted waiting for students to get materials ready, to start work, and to change tasks. Jess had complained often about not having time to fit every component of literacy into the allotted block, but he hadn't realized part of the problem was time lost making transitions. Jess shuddered to think of the amount of time that was slipping away every day.

During the post-observation consultation, his principal identified three skills for Jess to address: Time Limits, Cueing, and Proximity. They selected Time Limits as the starting point because it seemed to contribute most to lost time, as Jess's students did not know how long they had to start on work, how long they had for completing work, and how long for transitioning from one activity to the next. As a result, students felt no sense of urgency to be on task.

Jess's principal pointed out increases of student engagement during the few times Jess did give Time Limits, so they decided to focus on the literacy block

Time can be an elusive concept, certainly for children and sometimes for teachers. Nobody has trouble understanding that time exists for this or for that, but not all plan for the *amount of time* they have available for it. This is true in the broadest sense, not to get philosophical, and it is certainly true in the immediate sense of one's tasks at hand. Most people—especially children—need help recognizing the *limits of time* they have so they can complete tasks by focusing, planning, and applying.

Children need help focusing on *Time Limits*—the amount of time available to them for starting and completing a task. When inexperienced teachers ask students to perform something as simple as opening a book or beginning work on a project or a complex task like completing a timed essay, they may assume their students will begin immediately and will continue working until the task is completed. Without setting and monitoring **Time Limits**, however, these teachers inadvertently encourage poor habits. For instance, without help or reinforcement for focusing on Time Limits, some students never begin the task; others will not finish in time; many will experience frustration. Some may protest that they don't have enough time and are not finished, so their teacher, relieved that students actually wish to work on the task, allows them additional time. In effect, these students are taught that they do not have to begin tasks in a timely manner because their teacher will bend the rules for them. Or they decide that time doesn't matter. And, worse, they lose an opportunity to develop and improve their own time management skills.

The purpose of this chapter is to help you, the observer, recognize situations where children need more than their teacher's assumption that they can focus and manage time effectively. **Students need Time Limits to begin tasks and Time Limits to complete tasks. First and foremost, they need help understanding and practicing Time Limits** (Colvin, et al., 1997; Lane, et al., 2003; Lo, et al., 2002).

As an evaluator, you will find it important to recognize the elements of effective Time Limits and to recognize when a teacher needs help developing this skill.

Elements of Time Limits

You can expect that teachers who set Time Limits and monitor them effectively will have fewer discipline problems and achieve higher levels of student learning because more students will be on-task sooner and for longer periods of time.

Your teacher should set and monitor Time Limits throughout the instructional day. As you observe, keep in mind that certain Time Limits may have been set prior to your visit so you may be witnessing only your teacher's *monitoring* of Time Limits. This is fine, and it might be a topic for discussion during your debriefing.

In observations, look for two different kinds: procedural Time Limits and academic Time Limits. ***Procedural Time Limits,* those procedures teacher and students repeat systematically, will become habitual for students if they are set and then monitored consistently.**

CASE STUDY – *cont'd*

and to identify critical times for Jess to clarify the following Time Limits: First, how long students have to transition from one activity to another; second, how long students have to start work after receiving instructions; third, how long students have to complete tasks. The principal arranged to observe Jess over two days during literacy blocks.

On the next visit, Jess principal noted successful uses of Time Limits for starting and completing tasks because student engagement increased. However, Jess failed to give students Time Limits for transitioning from an activity into writers' workshops. A transition that should have taken no more than 1 minute took 5.

In the next consultation, Jess's set a goal to give students a clear Time Limit for transitioning while continuing to give students Time Limits for starting and completing work. After two days, the principal used a *Drop-In Tool* but before making the observation asked Jess to reiterate his Time Limits goal, which was threefold:

- Time Limits for starting work
- Time Limits for completing work
- Time Limit for transitioning.

Jess's principal switched to a coaching stance and asked his teacher to reflect on the degree to which he had achieved his Time Limits goal and to support his perception by using the data collected during the observations. Jess identified average engagement levels of 80% to 85% and improvements in levels for transitioning. Jess set a new goal to maintain progress with Time Limits, to refine transitions between all activities, and to extend his focus to include entire mornings. This led to more measurable improvement. Sharpening Time Limits enabled Jess to maximize time for productive learning. ♦♦♦

These are obvious examples of procedural Time Limits:

- Lining up for lunch or recess
- Getting out materials for instruction
- Transitioning from one physical location to another
- Moving from whole-class into partner or small group work
- Cleaning up

You probably will observe a range of classroom procedures, and you will decide if these move seamlessly or deteriorate into confusion or chaos. If the latter seems the case, you may need to explore some of the simple but critical steps your teacher can take to use Time Limits effectively. For instance, in a conference with your teacher, you might discuss procedural Time Limits as a combination of Expectations built by offering intermittent Cues. Explain that Time Limits begin as procedures and then—with practice and Cueing—Time Limits and time management become habits. **When establishing Time Limits, your teacher must consistently give Time Limits with Cueing to eventually establish the habit.**

The next chart offers examples of procedures that your teacher can make habitual by using Cueing and other verbiage to establish Time Limits. As with many of the eight engagement skills, what begins as a procedure can turn into an internalized habit if the teacher puts forth necessary time and effort to teach the procedure and then follow with practice and feedback until the habit gels. A habit is a high form of management because a teacher has consciously released power to students—in a constructive way, of course—and students, through practice and refinement, have skills and understanding that make them ready for this responsibility (see Chapter 4: Expectations.)

Turning Procedures Into Habits		
Procedural Expectation	**Using Procedural Verbiage for Time Limits**	**Maintaining Time Limits to Establish Habits**
Lining up for lunch	*"It is time for lunch!" You have 30 seconds to be ready to line up. I will know that you are ready when you are standing behind your desk—looking hungry!"*	*"It is time for lunch!" Whisper to me how long it will take you to line up quietly."* (Teacher uses Proximity and whispers Cues to students who need assistance.)
Getting out materials	*"You have 5 seconds to have your math book open to page 10. Five. . .Sarah has her book out, Four. . .Table 2 has their eyes on page 10, etc."*	*"Math books open to page 10, please."* (Teacher then uses a Cue such as holding up five fingers to remind students of the time limit.)

Turning Procedures Into Habits		
Transitioning	*"Students, you have 5 seconds to move quietly to the rug. Table 1. . .show us how to move quietly. Table 2. . .thank you for moving without talking. Everyone else, 5. . .thank you for walking, 4. . .those of you at the carpet already are doing a fabulous job, 3. . .I don't even need to say. . .2. . .1.*	*"Table 1. . .move quietly to the rug. Table 2. . .etc.* (Teacher utilizes Cueing and Proximity as necessary.)
Partner/group work	*"You have 10 seconds to begin discussing with your partner, using a whisper voice, why the main character ran away." 10. . .Ellen and Gary are quietly discussing, 8. . .Sam and Seth are thinking. . . etc.*	*"Please discuss with your partner why the main character ran away. As soon as you have gathered your thoughts and are ready to discuss, give your partner a thumbs-up."*
Clean Up	*"It is time to clean up. Look at your area and picture what it will look like when it is clean. You have 5 seconds to be started. Five. . .The library center is putting books away, Four. . .the drama center is putting the costumes back in the box, etc."*	*"Time to clean up—look around your area. Picture what it will look like when it is clean. Look around—show me with your fingers how long you think it will take you to clean up your area."*

You might make a point of distinguishing *academic Time Limits* from procedural ones, as the former are embedded in your teacher's content lesson verbiage. A simple example you might use is one about Time Limits to complete an assignment and Time Limits to start an assignment. For instance, *"You will have 20 minutes to complete this math assignment. You will have 5 seconds to be working. Five. . .Josh is already focused on his math. Four. . .Sally has written down the first problem, etc."* More complex academic Time Limits at upper grades—ones that you might observe as part of student/teacher interaction during a lesson—could include starting- and ending-times for writing a brief description following a science demonstration or for taking notes prior to offering a critical position on a topic.

Go into your observation with the notion that every students nearly always needs Time Limits for completing an assignment, particularly one that is performed during the class session. Such a Time Limit needs to be given verbally and, sometimes, demonstrated in a visual way as well. Visual support may include timers, completion times on the board, or other graphic organizers to depict the finite nature of a specific period of time. A Time Limit to begin an assignment should become procedural, a habit, keeping in mind that some individual students may always need extra support to be successful at beginning a task.

Recognizing Successful Uses of Time Limits

When you see Time Limits used properly, you will see very little wasted class time. Teachers may even appear happier because they are not chasing unfocused or off-track behavior. Students appear more focused and comfortable because boundaries have been established. Here are a few examples of Time Limits set effectively:

Example 1: Kindergarten Time Limit to Begin Working in Centers

Mrs. Williams' kindergarten students are at the rug receiving instructions for working in centers. Using her customary teacher voice, Mrs. Williams tells her students, *"You will have 20 minutes in centers today"* even though her kindergarten students don't know exactly what 20 minutes means. Knowing this, Mrs. Williams uses an egg timer to help children visualize that the time is elapsing in a countdown. In fact, Mrs. Williams uses the phrase, *"Notice that the timer gives us a countdown, like right before a rocket launch."* As the teacher releases students to their centers, she directs them in a whisper-voice, *"I am looking for students who are working hard in 5 seconds. Five. . .Joycelynn is already at her center. Four. . .Samuel is tiptoeing to his center. Three. . .Bill has his hands to himself. Two. . .Students in the library center are all working. One. . .(in a very soft whisper)Everyone is focused."*

Something important to note is that Mrs. Williams uses a process that includes at least three engagement skills to help her set Time Limits: She uses Cueing to clarify her Expectations, and she uses Proximity to encourage a few students to focus on their center. Her use of Voice variations (Chapter 11) helps her manage the process: She uses her normal instructional volume and tone—her teacher voice—to present directions, and then she uses her whisper-voice to guide and reinforce students.

Example 2: 4th Grade Time Limit

Mr. LaMer has provided explicit instructions as well as guided practice with his students on letter writing explaining that each child will write a letter to a parent or grandparent. Confident that his students understand these Expectations, Mr. LaMer tells them that they will have 15 minutes to write a first draft of the letter, and he writes this number on the board to reinforce these Time Limits. Because it is November and his students have practiced Time Limits previously, Mr. LaMer also asks students to show him—by raising one finger per second—just how long they will need to begin writing. By doing this, he has used Signaling to help clarify Time Limits. Most students raise five fingers to Signal five seconds. Mr. LaMer moves toward the student who is Signaling 10 seconds over and over. Mr. LaMer provides whispered Cueing to individual students to reinforce this five second Time Limit. *"Seth, wow! You were started in three seconds." "Alex, four seconds. . .way to focus!"*

The observer notes that students have been well on task writing their letters. As the 15–minute Time Limit is rapidly approaching, Mr. LaMer can see that students will need more time. Mr. LaMer had suspected that this activity would become a 20– or 25–minute assignment, but he did not want to overwhelm some students with the longer time frame. To adjust Time Limits, Mr. LaMer then whispers to each table of students, *"How much more time do you think you will need?"* The teacher makes an executive decision and then returns to each table whispering, *"You have an additional 10 minutes. Thank you for working so hard! You have definitely earned this extra time."*

Recognizing Missed Opportunities

When establishing a procedure, particularly at the beginning of the school year, teachers may need to provide Time Limits and behavioral Expectations with many or most directions. For example, *"You will have 5 seconds to quietly begin working on your math assignment."* Cueing can add important support for Time Limits. Here's a Cue that uses a countdown:

> *5. . .I see Joyceln is writing. 4. . .Bob is really thinking. 3. . .Table 5, you are ALL on task; please give yourselves 5 bonus points."*

The chart that follows illustrates a few examples of ineffective directions that can be remedied by Time Limits. Notice that even though the directions are reasonably clear, missing elements may cause management problems.

Opportunities for Improving Time Limits

Directions	Time Limit Failure	Time Limit Solution
"Your assignment today is to do problems 1 to 20."	Students don't know when to begin or how long they have to complete the 20 problems of an assignment. No Time Limits are given.	Give students a Time Limit for completing the assignment. *"Students, you have 20 minutes to complete problems 1 to 20 on page 129."*
"You have 30 minutes to complete problems 1 to 20."	Students are not given a Time Limit to begin working. Many students are not working after 10 minutes have passed.	Give a Time Limit to start the assignment and to complete it. *"Students I will give you 30 minutes to complete problems 1 to 20 on page 129. You have 15 seconds to be started."*
"Line up for lunch."	Students are not given a Time Limit to line up for lunch.	Give students a Time Limit for being lined up for lunch. *"Students, when I snap my fingers twice, you have 15 seconds to be quietly lined up for lunch."*
"Open your books to page 10. You have 5 seconds."	A Time Limit is given but is not supported with Cues.	After giving the five second Time Limit, count down from 5 to 1 offering a positive Cue between each number. *"5. . .Sophia has already opened her book, 4. . .Thank you, Boris, for quietly turning your pages, 3. . .Everyone on table three has the book turned to page 10."*

Consulting for Time Limits

Keep in mind that Time Limits are verbal directions, for the most part, given by the teacher. The ways in which your teacher establishes Time Limits will affect student behaviors, so you will want to be alert to students' responses. Carefully noting student engagement will help you (1) determine whether a problem exists with your teacher's directions, (2) identify strengths and weaknesses in your teacher's mastery of Time Limits, and (3) begin a process of helping your teacher develop this skill.

The model on this page demonstrates a principal's observation notes finding this teacher competent in all but one area of using Cueing to reinforce Expectations during a Time Limit countdown. In this case, the principal notes only one *Polisher*, posed as a question, for moving forward.

Time Limits Focused Observation Tool

Name: S Sundleman Date: 10/26/09
Grade/Subject: 4 Observer: J. Pit

Time Limit: Teacher identifies and communicates specific times for beginning and completing tasks

Directions: Place a rating in the appropriate column

✓ = Competent example of Time Limits
✓+ = Excellent example of Time Limits
✓– = Ineffective example of Time Limits

The teacher . . .

✓	gives a Time Limit to complete tasks
✓	gives a Time Limit to begin tasks
–	uses Cues to reinforce Time Limits (e.g., "You have 5 seconds to begin 5. . .I see Josh is already started 4. . .Amanda has her pencil moving,. . .")

Observation Notes:

Keepers:

You gave students a time limit to complete the task and one to begin the task!

Polishers:

How could you use Cueing during a count down to reinforce your Expectations?

Reproducible: Page 178, Appendix

Other Strategies for Consulting about Time Limits

You have options for consulting in depth with your teacher, helping to identify specific tactics and strategies for employing Time Limits in the classroom.

Option 1: Use a Depth Observation Tool

Use a *Depth Observation Tool* for Time Limits to collect data that provides specific feedback of actual verbiage your teacher uses. This tool also tracks the ways students respond to their teacher's directions and support.

To use a *Depth Observation Tool* for Time Limits, follow these steps:

1. Script your teacher's Time Limits in the first column labeled Time Limit.
2. For each Time Limit you enter, note the teacher's support behavior(s) in the second column labeled *Teacher Support*.
3. Describe the students' responses in the third column labeled *Student Response*.
4. Record the percentage of students who respond appropriately in the fourth column.

Time Limits Depth Observation Tool

Name: *Rachelle Wu* Date: *12/3/09*

Grade/Subject: *4th Math* Observer: *Janet Thorpe*

Directions:

- Script your teacher's Time Limits in the column labeled "Direction."
- For each Time Limit you enter, note the teacher's support behavior(s).
- Describe the "Student Response" in the column to its right.
- Note the percentage of students who respond appropriately.

Direction That Could Include a Time Limit (Script the Teacher)	Teacher Support (e.g., Proximity, Cueing)	Student Response	%
Open your books (how long?)		*Some open books. Some rummage. Others do nothing.*	*50*
Five seconds to find page 27.	*5. . .I see Bob has his book open. 4. . .Sally is finding it. 3. . .Table A is ready to go!*	*Students begin searching for the page and making eye contact with the teacher.*	*90*
Please work through the first ten problems. You will have 15 minutes (how long to begin?).	*Proximity is used for the nonstarters, but there are too many to get around to.*	*5 students begin. 10 students chat. 5 students rummage in desks. 2 wander.*	*25*
I need you to start NOW! Right NOW—I mean it if you don't want homework.	*(Cues?)*	*A few more start. . .*	*50 75*
The timer goes off—Ok, students give me a thumbs-up if you are finished.		*50% thumbs-up. 50% thumbs-down. We need more time.*	*80*
You will have 5 seconds to be started if you would like 5 additional minutes. If you are done, you may do a fast-finisher activity.	*5. . .Jocelyn is already started. 4. . .Bobby is started on a fast-finisher. 3. . .Ellen is focused on the task.*	*Students begin working on the task or on a fast finisher.*	*95*

Observation Notes:

Keepers:

When you gave specific Time Limits and followed them up with Cueing, 95% of your students responded. Impressive!

Polishers:

How can you remember to give Time Limits to start and finish tasks?

How can you employ Proximity as you reinforce your Time Limits?

Reproducible: Page 179, Appendix

The example above shows data collected on a *Depth Observation Tool* for Time Limits. In a post-observation conference, Principal Thorpe drew Wu's attention to the high levels of student engagement (90% and 95%) during two intervals in which she'd given Time Limit Expectations and followed them up with a countdown of five giving a positive Cue between each number. She commented on those under *Keepers* and noted one *Polisher* in the form of a question: *How can you remind yourself to give Time Limits to start and finish tasks?* By containing the number of *Polishers* to two, Principal Thorpe helps Wu set a reasonable goal that will help her further master Time Limits without feeling overwhelmed while realizing that this teacher is ready to work on more than one engagement skill.

Option 2: Guide Your Teacher through a Demo Observation

If possible, have your teacher use a *Demo Observation Tool* for Time Limits like the one below so that he or she may (1) identify specific uses of Time Limits by the demonstration teacher, (2) enter a brief description of each use of Time Limits, and (3) note the student response for each teacher action. Be sure to ask your teacher to describe the resulting effects of each use of Time Limits on student behavior. Discuss specific language, such as words in a countdown, as you consult following the focused observation. In addition, help your teacher set goals for whichever elements of Time Limits he or she chooses to transfer into the classroom.

In this example of a completed tool for observing a demonstration teacher. In this example, Ms. Sundleman and her administrator have observed Mrs. Cole's fourth grade for the purpose of capturing engagement skills that support Time Limits.

Time Limits
Demo Observation Tool

Observer: *Miss Sundleman* Grade/Class: *4th Grade self-cont*
Demo Teacher: *Ms. Helen Cole* Date/Time: *11/12/09*

Skill Definitions: Teacher identifies and communicates specific times for beginning and completing tasks

Directions: Write examples of your demonstration teacher's Time Limits in the first column. Then, for each Time Limit you enter, note the teacher's support behavior(s) and describe the "Student Response" in the column to its right

Time Limit (Script the Teacher)	Teacher Support Behaviors			Student Response
	Cueing	Proximity	Signals	
You have 10 seconds to open your math books to page 5. Give me a thumbs-up when you are ready!	*5. . .Thank you, Bill for being so fast.*	*Moving toward Sam, who is off task.*	*Give me a thumbs-up when you are ready!*	*90% of students responded within the 5 seconds. The two students who didn't responded immediately when Mrs. Cole used Proximity.*
Whisper to your neighbor how you think you should solve this problem. You will have 30 seconds.	*Whispered, "Wow, you are really discussing!" Thumbs-up to Sam.*	*Constant eye contact with Sam.*		*85% of students discuss the math problem.* *Sam (once he felt Mrs. Cole's eyes) immediately began discussing with his partner.*
White boards up in 10 seconds.	*3. . .Sam's marker is down. 2. . .Table 5 is ready. . .*	*Moving around during the first 5 seconds.*	*White boards up!*	*100% of students showed their boards on the cue.*
You have 20 minutes to complete this assignment. (Teacher set a visual timer.)				*Nodding.*
You have 10 seconds to be working.	*5. . .WOW! Table 3 has great focus. 4. . .Jill's eyes are on her book. 3. . .I hear pencils working. . .*	*Moving around during first 5 sec toward Sam.*		*80% of kids were started in the first 5 seconds. After the cues, all but Sam were started.*

Teacher Transfer: In my classroom, I want to set and refine this Expectation:

1. *Use Time Limits even for quick things like opening a book, whispering to a neighbor.*
2. *Follow up Time Limits with Cueing and Proximity–especially proximity.*

Reproducible: Page 180, Appendix

Option 3: Shadow Your Teacher for Time Limits

Intervene as needed to help your teacher identify opportunities for applying Time Limits. For instance, you might offer informational Cues such as *"How much time do students understand they have for getting started?"* You can offer specific directions like *"Give a 5–second Time Limit,"* or *"Use Cueing during your countdown."*

As your teacher responds to your informational Cues, you can switch to using Signals from a greater distance like from the back of the room. In advance of a shadowing session, you may identify Signals like these:

Using Signals for Shadowing Time Limits	
Signal	**Indication**
Point to a clock or to your wristwatch.	Give a Time Limit.
Thumbs-up.	Use Cueing during a Time Limit for beginning a task (e.g. a countdown).
Back of hand to mouth.	Whisper reinforcement or additional directive.

Coaching for Time Limits

Be sure not to use your coaching stance until your teacher has a basic understanding of Time Limits. Assist your teacher in visualizing specific Time Limit opportunities that may present themselves in an upcoming lesson that you will observe. Help your teacher identify places in the upcoming lesson that will require conscious efforts to employ Time Limits and to suggest tactics that will help students remain cognizant of time. Following are some possible questions that you can use to encourage and assist your teacher:

Coaching Conversation for Time Limits
Questions for Planning a Visit and Observation

- What is your goal for using Time Limits during your lesson?
- Walk me through your lesson. What opportunities do you see for using Time Limits? How long will students have to complete ______? How long will students have to begin working on ______?
- What will your Cueing sound like to reinforce your Time Limits? Give me an example.
- What behavioral problems do you foresee? How can you use Time Limits to curtail these possible situations?
- How will you know if your use of Time Limits is successful?

Time Limits Coaching Tool

Name: Emily Tate Date: 12/17/09
Grade/Subject: 1st Observer: Avery, prin.

Time Limit (Script the Teacher)	Teacher Action (e.g., Cueing, Proximity, Signals)	Student Response	%
You have 20 seconds to transition to the rug.	Cueing during countdown.	Students moving. Some are chatting. Two push chairs.	70
Eyes on me in 5 seconds.	Signal: thumbs-up.	All but Isaac and Emily focus on teacher by the count of 4.	90
White boards on your laps and ready to write in 15 seconds. Give me a thumbs-up when you are ready!		Most students respond rapidly.	80
White boards. . .SHOW!	Proximity toward Zach. Cueing: 5. . .Sam is ready to show when I give the signal. 4. . .Julie is ready, waiting for the signal.	Some write, some talk, some continue to work.	50
White boards. . .Show in 20 seconds when I say SHOW!		Students show white boards on "show."	95
Move back to your desks.	Proximity Cueing	Running, pushing, tipping over chairs, talking, etc.	10
Let's try that again (has students return to the rug.) I will be looking for tiptoeing 1st graders who can show me they are at their desks and ready in 20 seconds.		Tiptoeing: Some remind others with a whispered shhh.	95

Reproducible: Page 181, Appendix

"Why are my Time Limits sometimes effective and sometimes not?" Mrs. Tate wanted to know, so she asked her principal to help her find answers. On the left is the tool her principal used to collect data to aid in coaching.

Notice in the data that when Ms. Tate incorporates a Signal or a Cue with her Time Limit, her students respond with no lesson delay. However, when the teacher does not support her Time Limit with Cueing or Proximity, her student responses lag.

The principal left this tool behind and asked her teacher to note patterns that she saw. In follow-up, she scheduled a reflective conversation:

Reflective Conversation Questions Following the Visit and Observation

- How did it go? Did you meet your goal with Time Limits? How do you know?
- Did your plans to utilize Time Limits go as planned? Why or why not?
- What patterns do you see in the data I shared with you?
- What does this data tell you about your use of Time Limits?
- What did you learn about Time Limits that you want to replicate every time you teach?
- What ONE thing do you want to refine further in your use of Time Limits?

Chapter 10

Tasking

Skill #7

The Big Eight Engagement Skills

EXPECTATIONS
ATTENTION PROMPTS
PROXIMITY
CUEING
SIGNALS
TIME LIMITS
Tasking Teacher focuses and sharpens students' engagement through questioning strategies, purposeful and thought-provoking activities, and other tactics to direct their learning.
VOICE

10

Tasking

Skill #7

TOOLS for Evaluating TASKING

See Appendix pages. 182–186

CASE STUDY

I observed Laura's 8th grade direct instruction math lesson. Her engagement percentage was a paltry 15%. Students chatted, wandered, played at their desks.

Although Laura had problems with Cueing, Proximity, Attention Prompts, Signals, Time Limits, and Expectations, my data revealed that Tasking seemed to be the most problematic for this teacher.

"As I observed you today," I began my debriefing, *"I watched for what bothers you. It became apparent you were uncomfortable during direct instruction when students were not focused."*

I highlighted the lines of the data that related only to Tasking. Laura recognized that her open questions confused most students. Some called out, which led to more call-outs, but most students simply did not respond.

Together, Laura and I worked on her questioning by introducing a Signal for students to know when to raise their hands or to respond chorally.

The next day, as I observed, Laura Signaled students at every question, and more students responded. Later, we discussed

It's probably a no-brainer that students don't like to be bored, which can be a good thing or a bad thing depending on how well a teacher engages students and channels their interests. As any experienced teacher knows, students will find things to do—unconstructive or even disruptive things—when their time and their minds are not constructively engaged. Students who are not on task may be students who are getting into trouble of some kind or, worse, students who simply are not learning. Accordingly, it is every teacher's responsibility to direct every and all students toward constructive endeavor. Several researchers have found that when students are actively engaged in learning processes, both on-task behaviors and academic achievement increase (Carnine, et al., 2004; Godfrey, et al., 2003; Greenwood, et al., 2002; Sutherland, et al., 2003).

***Tasking* involves teacher-made directions offered in clear and timely fashion so that students remain actively engaged in their own learning. In effect, the teacher sees to it that students are working constructively.**

Effective teachers find specific tactics for engaging their students by planning lessons that will involve students as active participants, not as passive learners. Jane Vella (2001), author of *Taking Learning to Task*, advises that we learn what we do. Nationally recognized experts in processes for improving adult and student learning, DuFour,

Dufour, Eaker, and Many (2006, p. 2) assert, *"We learn best by doing."* A reasonable minimum goal for every teacher is to achieve 80% or better of active student engagement. Each teacher has not only the power but also the obligation to use **Tasking** skills to reach such a benchmark and to maintain the level at all times.

Tasking is a critical skill every teacher needs to hone. We urge evaluators to recognize the elements of Tasking, to look for Tasking during classroom observations, and to recognize teachers' needs in developing this skill further.

CASE STUDY – *cont'd*

three kinds of questioning. I reminded Laura of my first observation and noted that she had asked 5 assessment, 10 open, but zero engagement questions. Even worse, Laura answered her own questions five times.

As a result, Laura set the goal to reduce her open questions to no more than five, to quit answering her own questions, and to increase her engagement questions to at least five. She set about thinking of wordings she planned to use in her next lessons.

Three days later, my data showed Laura had indeed met her goal as her on-task engagement increased to 80%! She declared proudly that she was developing the habit of preparing engagement questions before every lesson.

By achieving success in one area, Laura became more able to believe she could become a good teacher.

One year later, her colleagues selected her team demonstration teacher—for Tasking!

—A. Verhaal, Principal

Recognizing the Need for Tasking

In any classroom situation, it might be a safe bet that the children have an innate desire to please their teacher and to respond in ways that earn positive feedback or results. **Problems occur when students do not know what is expected of them and when teachers have not asked the right questions or provided an engaging Task.**

As an observer, you will become concerned if children appear not to know what their teacher wants. Does my teacher want students to call out or raise their hands to respond to questions? What does my teacher want students to do when they are ready to participate?

Be on the lookout for the following cycle of problems: A teacher asks a question. Some students raise their hands to respond. Some call out. The teacher responds to one child who has called out, which encourages other students to call out. The classroom is noisy and becomes noisier. Some students do appear engaged, but many others appear distracted or engaged in unrelated activity. The teacher's voice rises. Children's voices rise. The observer pops an aspirin.

In your debriefing, you may need to remind your teacher that kids like to know what is expected of them and that each teacher has not only the power but also the obligation to use Tasking among their other engagement skills. Remind them that Tasking helps communicate Expectations clearly and effectively.

For instance, you might ask your teacher if students know when to call out or raise their hands during direct instruction. That may lead you to ask if your teacher has clarified a response method like a Signal for children *before* they answer a question (e.g., *"Raise your hand if you know the name of the story's narrator?"*) Or you might ask if, during guided practice, your teacher engages students actively (e.g., writing on white boards, working with partners, keeping a tally sheet).

Recognizing Elements of Tasking

Because Tasking facilitates instructional routines, this skill is an integral part of lesson sequencing. **Elements of Tasking include (1) Signals during direct instruction, (2) engagement-based questioning and activity during direct instruction and guided practice, and (3) lesson planning for student engagement during direct instruction, guided practice, and independent practice.**

Be alert for the kinds of questions and directions your teacher offers during instruction. These are a few examples of deficient and effective Tasking you may observe:

Recognizing Tasking During Instruction

Instructional Strategy	Deficient Tasking	Effective Tasking
Direct Instruction: Lesson calls for students to respond chorally.	Teacher asks questions but provides few Cues to respond (even if one or two students answer questions).	Teacher prompts students by raising and then lowering an arm for them to respond chorally to a question.
Guided Practice	Teacher moves from lecture to independent practice without actually guiding practice.	Teacher has students solve problem on individual white boards and show their answers on Cue.
Independent Practice	Students work without assistance, some possibly making errors that are not made known to the teacher or other monitor.	Teacher has students sign their names on the board when they are ready for the teacher or other monitor to check their answers.

Tasking and Questioning

Teachers who Task students effectively know how to ask questions that get students thinking and involved in the essential aspects of the concepts or skills at hand. **The questions teachers ask are, in effect, the shapers and shepherds of the dialogue between them. You will easily spot three varieties of questions that elicit vastly different rates of student involvement. Look for these three types of questions—or directions—during your observations:**

Assessment Questions

Open Questions

Engagement Questions

You probably will notice also that different types of questions result in very different rates of responses, with engagement questions eliciting the highest rates and assessment types of questions eliciting the lowest:

Assessment Questions

Adroit management of assessment questions helps students unlearn the practice of invisibility, or "hiding" from questions. Too often, students as young as first graders learn that if they don't raise their hands when questions are asked, they avoid an Expectation to focus—that is, they avoid being part of the learning process.

A teacher may use an assessment question as a way of catching a student off-guard or, worse, to embarrass a student who appears not to have been paying attention. This practice can stagnate or deteriorate the classroom environment.

Assessment questions do serve a limited purpose, but the weakness of assessment questions is that they require only one student to respond—the student to whom the question is directed. In a classroom of 25 students, for instance, that leaves 24 who are unengaged and many perhaps not thinking about what it is they need to know or be able to do. A teacher may fall into a trap with assessment questions by using this device too frequently to check that students are paying attention or that they have done their work, or if they continually ask assessment questions of the same students they feel certain will offer the correct answers. Imagine a full 20– or 30–minute lesson in which only one student is asked to respond at a time; many other students may sit quietly, but the likelihood exists that their minds will wander because others are doing the heavy lifting.

A wise approach is to use *assessment questions* sparingly as quick checks into students' comprehension during lessons. In particular, assessment questions are most engaging when students are chosen by a system of chance, such as by drawing names or by using computer generated randomizers or just by a teacher's body language meant to imply randomness. If a student *does not know* whether or not he will be called on, the more attention he will likely pay to the question.

The basic rule of thumb for asking assessment questions is to engage all students and then to assess one student. Here is an example of Tasking directions from a 7th grade English classroom teacher during a whole-group literature discussion:

Example: Directions for Tasking
Who was the MOST conflicted character in the story and why?
Table 3, prepare to answer.
Table 4, Member 3, what is your answer?

Open Questions

Because some questions may be too broad or open-ended, they leave students out of the process of engaged learning. This type of questioning generally elicits responses from only about 30% of students because open questions tend to be poorly constructed ones that leave students confused or else unsure about how to respond to their teacher. **A reason for your teacher to avoid overuse of open questions is because these are broad-brush, too general, or vaguely phrased in the mistaken notion that an open-ended question will**

spark creative thinking or even excitement. For instance, a question like "*What did you think about that story?*" may seem harmless and, indeed, some excitable students might pipe up with personal responses or anecdotes of their own, but the time spent in this manner may be aimless or digressive. Even if the teacher does want to know how students feel about the story, the question is ineffective because it doesn't require students to interact with the text in any particular way, nor does it give students an appropriate or focused way to respond. With only 30% of students responding to such questions, 70% of students may be listening but probably are not formulating engaged connections to the matter at hand—specifically, to the aspects of the story itself. Some students may truly enjoy venting their thoughts and feelings, but for others the act of listening is not active engagement.

Engagement Questions

These may not be possible, or even advisable, 100% of the time, but they should indeed be the principal questioning strategy of your teacher. Using the example of students arriving in class to discuss a new story, let's look at constructing questions that lead students to interact with the text in purposeful ways. **An engagement question achieves at least two immediate goals: (1) It narrows students' focus to a particular aspect, and (2) it embeds some personal investment on the part of every student into the process of answering the question. Even embedding words like "*Think first before you answer. . .*" engages students in a personal way.** Here's another example: A teacher may phrase a question like this: "*You have two minutes to think about, or list in your notes, three specific things you either liked or disliked about this story.*" From such a point, discussion can proceed from thoughtful, engaged behavior rather than from top-of-mind or arbitrary stimuli. **Sharpened engagement yields deeper learning.**

Here are more specific examples of these three types of questioning you may observe your teacher using during instruction:

Types Of Questions During Instruction

Question Type Defined	Example of Question Type	Response Rate
Assessment Question: Teacher directs question to one student for one response.	*Deyanne, who is the main character in this story?*	5%
Open Question: Teacher fishes for answers by asking an open-ended or overly-general question, typically with urgency or by offering little wait-time.	*Quick! Who are the main characters?* *What happened on p. 13?* *What is the answer to no. 7?*	30%–40%
Engagement Question: Teacher provides response mechanism in question phrasing, such as a Signal or physical Cue or thought-provoker to help students formulate answers.	*Show me a finger count for how many characters are in the story.* *Whisper to your neighbor the main characters in the story.*	90%–100%

During direct instruction, your teacher's goal should be 70% of that time devoted to engagement questions and no more than 30% spent on assessment questions. While a teacher may feel that open questions spark students' interests, he or she may have a point but only on rare occasions as an anticipatory set—if at all.

It may be important for you, the evaluator, to distinguish effective questioning (Tasking) from open questioning. The teacher who asks open questions typically will have a response engagement rate not exceeding 30% during direct instruction. The obvious result is that too few students are actively engaged, but the problem may extend further. A Tasking failure in one or two classes may have an adverse ripple effect across a grade. Consider this true experience: A consultant in a small junior/senior high school made engagement observations with the school coach and an administrator and came across a classroom in which the teacher allowed three bright and eager students to carry the discussion and to volunteer all answers. The consultant decided to follow the same group of students to their other classes and discovered in every class the same three students answered most questions. It was as if these three students had been assigned, or had assumed, the role of question answerers for their classmates. Both the consultant and the administrator concluded that the problem could be addressed by coaching several teachers in the team to Task for the purpose of engaging many more students.

Keep in mind that different kinds of questions have different rates of response, which suggests that certain questions like engagement-type questions are more fruitful (90%) than open questions (30%) or assessment questions (5%.)

Typically, a problem with open questioning is that many or most students will not know how to respond to the question, hence a 30% response rate meaning that less than a third of students will think of, or will be able to offer, a correct answer.

A worthwhile goal for some teachers is to rephrase open and assessment questions as engagement-type questions. Following are a few more examples you might use in consultations about Tasking. Take notice of the questions in the left column, which are random and assessment-type questions. Alongside each, in the far right column, is essentially the same request repositioned as an engagement question. For a teacher who struggles with questioning for engagement, or with Tasking generally, this chart may offer useful clarifications:

Moving toward Engagement Questions

Question/Request	Type of Question	Rephrased for Engagement
What is the main character thinking?	Open	*Whisper to your neighbor what you think the main character is thinking.*
Which spelling is correct?	Open	*Here are two spellings for the word. Raise your left hand if you think the first is correct, your right hand if you think it's the second spelling.*
Ellen, what is the capital of Utah?	Assessment	*Think.* (Teacher holds hand in stop position.). . .*What is the capital of Utah?. . .Think.* (Teacher drops the arm and asks for responses.)

Recognizing Successful Uses of Tasking

Teachers who use Tasking to great advantage typically have well-thought-out, engaging lessons. A teacher who has planned specifically for Tasking, and who enjoys active student engagement, typically will have far fewer behavioral problems than a teacher who is attempting to teach ad hoc or without a well-defined plan.

Try to recall a teacher from your own schooldays—one who mastered *Tasking*. (This might be hard for you to remember because you were probably quite busy!) But if you can bring one to mind, you might be thinking of a class that had not been easy but one you learned from—one in which you felt purposeful and had a sense that you were learning.

Undoubtedly, you will carry your own visions of good Taskers into your classroom observations. Here are a few more examples:

Examples of Tasking		
Instructional Strategy	**Strategies for Tasking**	**Examples of Tactics for Tasking**
Direct Instruction	Teacher gives the method of response before the question.	*Give a thumbs-up if you know the capital of Virginia.* *Write your answer in the air for 18 + 2.* *Show me (with a finger count) how many words you can think of that rhyme with cat.* *Touch your nose if you know how many syllables there are in the word hippopotamus.*
Direct Instruction	Teacher prompts for choral response.	*Think* (teacher holds hand in stop position). . .*of a time that you were a loyal friend. . .think, whisper to your neighbor* (teacher drops her hand down).
Guided Practice	Teacher engages students with white boards.	*Write your answer to 18+2 on your white board. Hold it up when I prompt you.*
Guided Practice	Teacher utilizes Partner-Share.	*Whisper to your neighbor what you think our main character will do next. As soon as you agree, show me a thumbs-up.*
Guided Practice	Teacher manages group-think.	*Person #1: Write the equation on your paper.* *Person #2: Factor the quadratic.* *Person #3: Solve each factor [set = to 0].* *Person #4: Write the answer in the form of 2 points.* *Person #1: Sketch the graph of the quadratic.*

Tasking Planning Guide

Name: *Elaine Smith* Date: *11/5/09*
Gradet: *1st* Topic: *Introduction to Fractions*

Directions: Use this tool to plan steps, procedures, and specific questions for upcoming lessons (Teacher DO) as well as the performance you expect (Student DO).

Teacher DO	Student DO
Direct Instruction: *Use samples to present new information on fractions.* *1. ½ of a candy bar (Hershey's–squares)* *2. ¼ of a candy bar (Hershey's–squares)* *3. ½ of a Kit-Kat* *4. ¼ of a Kit-Kat* *Which would you rather have?*	*During direct instruction, students will each have a card with ½ and ¼ on the sides. As I show a piece of candy bar, students will hold up their cards to show if the piece is ½ or ¼.* *Students will vote using their cards whether they would like to have ½ or ¼. They will huddle as a table to decide which they would rather have and why. I will call on person #3 from each table to share their answers.*
Guided Practice: *Provide each table of students with the following items: candy bar, 10 pennies, 1 cup of water, ½ and ¼ measuring cups.* *Check off each group for each problem. Note students who are having problems to meet with during independent practice.*	*Divide each item in ½.* *Divide each item in ¼.* *Group-Think: Describe what ½ means. Describe what ¼ means. Be ready to share one of your definitions with the class.*
Independent Practice: *Each student will have a practice sheet showing the following shapes: circle, square, rectangle and the following amounts of pennies: 20, 10, 4.* *Work with students who have problems with the check-off.*	*Divide each item in ½ and ¼. Do #1 (circle) and #4 (20 pennies) first. Please sign up on the board for check-off when you have finished these.* *Students will then finish the remainder of the sheet independently.*

Reproducible: Page 182, Appendix

To help your teacher plan for Tasking, you might offer a *Tasking Planning Guide*. Your teacher may utilize this tool not only to plan what to do but also to indicate how students will be actively engaged during each part of the lesson. In the left column of the two models on this page, notice that the *Teacher Do* steps should be minimized, and the *Student Do* steps maximized as the teacher moves from direct instruction to independent practice.

Recognizing Missed Opportunities for Tasking

In some classrooms, you will find the teacher doing all the work. He writes the problems on the board, solves the problems, describes how he solved the problem, and then continues to do another problem with little or no input or feedback from students. This type of instructional routine, sometimes called a "stand and deliver classroom," often bores students because many of them simply are not learning.

Be on the lookout for other failures in Tasking. Following is not a complete list, yet it offers some frequent problems you may recognize.

Tasking in Classroom Situations

Classroom Situation	Tasking Failure	Solution
1. Teacher asks open questions. Students do not know how to respond.	Direct Instruction—Questioning	Engage students in whole class response before assessing one student.
2. Teacher lectures and then provides a worksheet.	Direct Instruction—Questioning Guided Practice	Use Tasking questions during direct instruction. Provide guided practice before independent.
3. Teacher has students respond with a thumbs-up or thumbs-down to all questions.	Lack of variety	Use a variety of tasking prompts and Signals: write in the air, whisper to your neighbor, etc.

Consulting for Tasking

Tasking is evidenced by active rather than passive student engagement. Paying attention to student behaviors will help you identify strengths and weaknesses in the teacher's mastery of Tasking skills.

Tools like the one to the right will help you focus on this skill. It identifies four teacher actions (in the middle of the tool) that can be evaluated by observing student activity. This model shows a principal's observation that a teacher is competent in all but one area of Tasking and needs help in using this skill during guided practice.

After a *Focused Observation*, you can use the tool for debriefing, pointing out the elements of Tasking performed well (plus one element to focus on.) Using a *Tasking Planning Guide (Teacher Do-Student Do)* might be a great next step for planning a subsequent visit for Tasking.

Tasking
Focused Observation Tool

Name: *Ms. Ishmel* Date: *2/9/09*
Grade/Subject: *7B* Observer: *Mr. Rough*

Time Limit: Teacher identifies and communicates specific times for beginning and completing tasks

Directions: Place a rating in the appropriate column

✓ = Competent example of Tasking
✓+ = Excellent or masterful example of Tasking
✓– = Ineffective attempt at Tasking

The teacher . . .

✓✓ ✓✓	uses various methods to keep students engaged during direct instruction (e.g., whisper to your neighbor, note taking guides, white boards)
✓✓	engages all students' thinking before one student responds
	provides guided practice including partner and group work
✓✓	utilizes active rather than passive engagement

Observation Notes:

Keepers:

Great use of a variety of kinesthetic student responses: touch your nose, write in the air, whisper to me, choral response on cue of your hand lowering, etc.

Polishers:

What type of guided practice would ensure student understanding before assigning independent practice?

Reproducible: Page 183, Appendix

Consulting in Greater Depth for Tasking

Additional tools and strategies exist for collecting more or more in-depth data in your consulting stance. Consider the following options.

Tasking Depth Observation Tool

Name: *Tim Frost* Date: *10/7/09*
Grade/Subject: *Sixth* Observer: *B. Donalds*

Directions:

1. Observe and record relevant teacher directions.
2. Describe the student response.
3. Estimate and note apparent percentage of students who respond appropriately.

Teacher Direction	Student Response	%
Think of the answer to 5+2/7. . . Think. . .Think. . .RESPOND	*Students wait to respond until the Cue is given and then respond, "1"*	*95*
Thumbs-up if my answer is correct, thumbs-down if incorrect. . . 5 × 2+7=14 On the count of three. . .1. . .2. . .3 SHOW	*Students waited until three and then responded with thumbs-down.*	*90*
Solve this problem on your white board—7 × 5 + 5 = . Be ready to show your board on the count of 10.	*Students show white boards. Three have incorrect answers.*	*95*
Solve this problem on your white board – 10 × 5 + 5 = . Be ready to show your board on the count of 10.	*Teacher moves toward three students who missed the last problem. Students show white boards.*	*95*

Observation Notes:

Keepers:

Your combination of using white boards and engagement questions is an excellent forum for focusing your students.

Polishers:

Continue to hone your Proximity skills as you monitor student performance on tasks.

Reproducible: Page 184, Appendix

Option 1: Guide Your Teacher through a Depth Observation

Here is a *Depth Observation Tool* that uses a *Teacher Direction/Student Response* feature for Tasking. It is a device for (1) recording your teacher's directions and questions as well as (2) student active responses during direct instruction.

In this model, Tim does well with Tasking, using Signals kinesthetically and for choral responses. He uses active engagement for guided practice by utilizing work boards for student responses. In the observer's debriefing with Tim, he might use the reflective coaching questions that follow in this chapter to facilitate his teacher's deeper thinking about the data.

In your debriefing with your teacher, be sure to identify each use of Tasking and to describe the resulting effects of each use of Tasking on student behavior.

Option 2: Guide Your Teacher through a Demo Observation

Choose a direct instruction lesson, if possible, for a Tasking demo. Have your teacher use the *Demo Observation Tool* for this observation and ask your teacher to complete it in these ways: (1) Identify specific uses of Tasking by the demonstration teacher, (2) enter a brief description of each use of Tasking according to its lesson element: *direct instruction, guided practice,* and *independent practice,* and (3) describe the student response for each teacher action.

Here is a model of a completed *Demo Observation Tool* for Tasking:

Tasking
Demo Observation Tool

Observer: Jane Elkin Grade/Class: 4th Grade self-cont.
Demo Teacher: Mrs. Helen McCool Date/Time: 05/20/09 10:25 am

Directions: Identify and describe specific uses of Tasking by the demonstration teacher. Be sure to enter these as questions or directions under the type of lesson: Direct Instruction, Guided Practice, Independent Practice. Then describe student response for each teacher action.

Direct Instruction		Guided Practice		Independent Practice	
Teacher Action	Student Response	Teacher Action	Student Response	Teacher Action	Student Response
Write the main character's name in the margine of your notes.	All students write in their notes.	Tchr assigns groups of 4 students with each student numbered 1 to 4.	Move to groups.	Assigns a task utilizing character trait analysis. Students are directed to check off their first two traits.	Begin working on the character trait sheet on the teacher's countdown of 3–see Sarah is already focused. 2–Sam is thinking, 1–Everyone is starting (said in a whisper voice).
Whisper to your partner how you know this person is the main character. Teacher moves towards stud's who are hesitant to respond.	Students whisper to partners.	Tchr asks variety of text questions for Group to answer. Teacher draws a number and that student for each group responds.	For each response, students instantly move into groups and ALL actively participate.		

Teacher Transfer: In my classroom, I want to focus on:

1. Utilize active engagement into my direct instruction. I can now see that my students are passive during this part of my lesson. I want to utilize tasking strategies such as: whisper to your neighbor, thumbs-up, response cards, white boards, etc.
2. Use group strategies for guided practice so that everyone participates, and I am also able to assess by having one student answer after they have all engaged.

Reproducible: Page 185, Appendix

Option 3: Shadow Your Teacher for Tasking during Direct Instruction

Shadowing provides real-time guided practice and gives you an opportunity to intervene as needed.

Keep in mind that shadowing for Tasking occurs on three levels: directing, guiding, and Signaling, as you see in the next chart. As your teacher responds to your guiding for Tasking, you can switch to Signaling from a greater distance—from the side or back of the room.

Shadowing for Tasking		
Technique	**Technique Defined**	**Examples of Statements for Tasking**
Directing	Shadower tells teacher exactly what to say in order to help teacher learn techniques and timing.	Say, *"Whisper to your neighbor, Alice."* Say, *"Class, write the answer in the air."* Say, *"Raise one finger for each idea you have."* Say, *"Respond on three. . .two. . .one. RESPOND."*
Guiding	Shadower asks teacher questions or gives broad directions to help teacher improve timing.	*"Can all students respond?"* *"Try phrasing your question so all students can respond."* *"Use an engagement question."*
Signaling	Shadower offers kinesthetic Signals from the back of the room as needed to remind teacher to use Cues or specific verbiage.	E.g., tapping of head.(prearranged Signal meaning "How can all students respond?")

Coaching for Tasking

Ask reflective questions that will help your teacher identify places in the upcoming lesson that will require conscious efforts to employ Tasking. Following are some questions you can use to encourage and assist the teacher in unlocking his or her own thinking as you work together.

Coaching Conversation for Tasking
Questions for Planning a Visit and Observation

- What is your Tasking goal during your lesson?
- What percentage of your questions will be engagement types?
- Walk me through your lesson.
  - Direct Instruction: How will students actively respond?
  - Guided Practice: How will students actively respond?
- What behavioral problems do you foresee? How can you use Tasking to curtail these possible situations?
- What will you see that will alert you to refocus your Tasking?
- How will you know if your Tasking is successful?

In addition, you might use some additional questions to facilitate your coaching dialogue. Consider providing your teacher with your observation data prior to this conversation.

Reflective Conversation Questions
Following the Visit and Observation

- How did it go? Did you meet your goal with Tasking? How do you know?
- What part of your lesson were students most engaged? What did you do that caused this to happen?
- Did your efforts to address active engagement go as planned? Why or why not?
- What patterns do you see in the data I shared with you?
- What does this data tell you about your uses of Tasking?
- What did you learn about Tasking that you want to replicate every time you teach?
- What ONE thing do you want to refine further about your Tasking skills?

Tasking Coaching Tool

Name: *Emily Tate* Date: *1st*
Grade/Subject: *Allison Avery, prin.* Observer: *12/17/09*

Directions: Script teacher's questions/directions for response in the appropriate column. During debriefing, coach the teacher to adjust verbiage to move into engagement column

Assessment Questions (Average 5% response)	**Open Questions** (Average 30% – 40% response)	**Engagement Questions** (Average 90% response)
One student/one response. Raise of hand—calling on one child, e.g., "Deyanne, who are the main characters?"	*"Fishing" for an answer. Students don't know how to respond. Question asked usually with no wait time. For example, "Who are the main characters?*	*1. Response method given before the question. "Show me (finger count) how many characters are in the story."* *2. Physical prompt to raise hand or respond chorally.*
Samantha, how do we begin a letter?	*Who knows what this (holding up a letter) is?*	*Stand up if you have ever received a letter!*
James, what is usually the first word in a friendly letter?	*What is wrong with this part of the letter?*	*Whisper to your neighbor who your letter was from.*
Sally, what do you think it is?	*Who could you send a letter to?*	*Write (in the air) how you would end this letter.*
James, why do you like getting letters?		*Heads together at your tables. Decide who your table is going to write a letter to? Then stand up behind your chairs so you can whisper the name to me. I will write it down!*

Reproducible: Page 186, Appendix

Here is yet another kind of data collection tool for coaching about Tasking. This one is used for teachers who want to analyze their own patterns of questioning. In this model, the administrator simply scripted the teacher's questions and directions in the appropriate column as to their type: open, assessment, or engagement. During the reflective conversation, the teacher can practice changing random questions to engagement types thus mentally rehearsing for the next lesson.

Chapter 11

Voice

Skill #8

The Big Eight Engagement Skills

EXPECTATIONS
ATTENTION PROMPTS
PROXIMITY
CUEING
SIGNALS
TIME LIMITS
TASKING

Voice

Teacher uses Voice to maximum effect: pitch in the lower registers, tone geared for situations, diction appropriate to students' age levels, and voice modulation, or cadence, to maintain interest.

11

Voice

Skill #8

TOOLS for Evaluating VOICE

See Appendix pages. 187–189

CASE STUDY

From *Drop-In* visits, Jan's principal recognized problems with his teacher's use of Voice, so he decided to use a *Focused Observation Tool.* He prearranged a visit following a debriefing in which Jan worried about too many of her students acting restless and engaging in side conversations nearly every time she began a lesson. *"No matter how loud I talk, some of my students just don't pay Attention. They don't listen, and I can't trust them to do the independent work."*

On the day Mr. Eggers observed for Voice, he found much to note on the tool—just as Jan had predicted!—but data from the tool provided Jan with some startling insights. For one, she didn't realize her Voice was so loud and harsh or that she tended to talk even louder and more rapidly as students became more restless. Second, she recognized that a teacher's Voice helps keep students engaged, and third she became unaware of specific techniques available for enhancing the effectiveness of her Voice.

Together, Jan and her principal decided to focus on two of the eight Voice techniques on the *Focused Observation Tool,* specifically (a) to pitch her voice in the

A teacher's **Voice** can be a strong asset or a glaring deficit. At its best, a well-developed classroom Voice can take children gently by the ears and hold them rapt (Gudmundsen, et al., 1996). Your teacher's Voice operates right on the front lines of your children's learning. Voice can keep students engaged in learning, calm noisy or restless students, convey information and directions, communicate authority and expertise and—very important—nurture relationships of respect and regard that honor students' ages and developmental levels. **Just as the classroom physical environment can inspire or bore children, *Voice* can be an affective environment—a portal that children navigate day by day and minute by minute influencing their Attention and feelings all along the way.**

As you observe for Voice, notice when a modulated or otherwise well-developed classroom Voice engages kids in ways that optimize their learning. You will see in an instant how some individuals possess naturally charismatic Voices and can employ them instinctively to great effect. Not all teachers are so fortunate, of course. **If teachers who struggle with Voice are willing to invest time and focus, they can develop Voices that will help them facilitate desirable outcomes—from commanding the inattentive to calming the excitable, from challenging the curious to inspiring the restless. And you can be of great help to them.**

Recognizing Successful Uses of Voice

Many master teachers credit their tone, diction, even stylistic devices for their ability to hold students' Attention during instruction or to manage students effectively through Tasks.

A skilled teacher directs Voice pitch to the lower registers where listening is more comfortable, being careful to project so students farther away can hear easily. In addition, the teacher subtly renews students' Attention by dropping Voice at the ends of sentences and then picks up pitch and volume to begin the next, striking a balance between an unhurried pace and an energy that engenders interest. The teacher incorporates these techniques so subtly that Voice does not compete with message (Gudmundsen, et al., 1996).

Another achievement of a Voice-wise teacher is demonstrating respect for students through tone and body language as well as the very words that deliver the message. **Civility is key, avoiding a sarcastic voice—even in the most stressful circumstances—and remaining mindful of students' ages and developmental levels.** This teacher knows that sarcasm communicates disrespect or disdain, which will ultimately undermine relationships with students. **Sarcasm has no place in the classroom.**

In short, teachers who master Voice become adept at using these elements to communicate in ways large and small:

Elements of Voice

Pitch	(sometimes called *register*, the highness or lowness of Voice)
Tone	(the *attitude*, or feeling, conveyed by sound of Voice)
Diction	(*language*, specific word choices)
Cadence	(*modulation* or dynamic movement of Voice upward as a question or downward in pitch to create interest and to promote Attention)

CASE STUDY – *cont'd*

low ranges, and (b) to drop her voice at the ends of sentences. Mr. Eggers suggested two events when she might incorporate the following techniques: reading aloud to the whole class (a low-stress situation) and reteaching a math concept (more stressful).

Jan's first attempt felt like a disaster to her. Students were more restless and off task than ever, so Mr. Eggers arranged for Jan to observe Ms. Wilson's Voice techniques with 5th grade, and together they collected data using a *Demo Observation Tool.* The demo helped Jan better understand Voice techniques, so she tried that very afternoon to pitch her Voice to lower ranges, even dropping her Voice at the ends of sentences. She discerned some increased engagement.

The next day, Mr. Eggers slipped in for 5 minutes, gave her a thumbs-up as she read aloud to students, and later they agreed he would observe another math lesson with the same tool they had used for the demo observation.

Yes, the next data showed increased engagement, so they decided to add the technique of pacing Voice at a relaxed rate. This is when Mr. Eggers switched to a coaching stance.

Subsequent coaching conversations included reflecting on new data and setting a goal to incorporate still more Voice techniques. Over the course of the year, Jan noted significant gains in her students' engagement and attributed much of those changes to her work on Voice.

This process gave Jan a system—and an inspiration—to work on improving other engagement strategies, so she asked her principal and a fellow teacher to collect data as she practiced techniques for other skills—Cueing, Signals, Tasking.

♦♦♦

Expect to hear some differences in uses of Voice at different grade levels. Here are two examples: A 1st grade teacher might occasionally choose a quiet Voice with exaggerated excitement using statements like *"Boys and girls, today our librarian is so very excited to be with you"* or *"Thank you, Johnny, for being such a quiet listener for Mrs. Peterson."* On the other hand, when guiding 6th grade students working independently, a teacher might use a well-modulated Voice that is calm and unhurried, using statements like *"Jody, thank you for moving so quickly into silent reading"* or *"Thank you, class. Your excellent comments tell me you were well prepared today for current events."*

The next chart offers you a summary of the major purposes of classroom Voice.

Purposes of Classroom Voice		
Purpose	**Ineffective Voice**	**Effective Voice**
Keep Students Engaged	Teacher speaks in a loud Voice that goes up at the end of each sentence. Volume increases to overcome distractions or to grab Attention.	Teacher uses a well-modulated Voice that projects so all students can hear and drops off at the ends of some sentences.
Calm Students	Teacher speaks to students in a relentlessly loud Voice that is irritating and causes students to be restless.	Teacher speaks in a relaxed Voice in the lower registers, infusing sufficient energy to project, while lowering volume gradually to settle students.
Convey Information and Give Directions	Teacher's Voice is shrill or has annoying attributes that compete with focus or cause students to lose focus on the information or on the teacher generally.	Teacher communicates information in a well-modulated Voice to hold focus without distracting from the message.
Communicate Authority and Expertise	Teacher uses an overly friendly Voice, which invites informal communication such as call-outs, or a hesitant Voice that projects lack of confidence.	Teacher speaks to students in a businesslike Voice that communicates expertise and authority.
Communicate Respect and Regard	Teacher infuses Voice with sarcasm or talks down to students using expression and phrasing that do not align with the age and developmental levels of the students.	Teacher uses diction (word choices) and tone (expressions of attitude) that are respectful and appropriate to the ages and developmental levels of students.

Following are some examples of teachers who use Voice to create environments that optimize student learning.

Example 1: Keeping 8th Grade Students Engaged in a General Science Lesson

Data now shows that Mindy regularly has 85% to 95% of her 8th grade students engaged during academic instruction, but this was not always the case. In her first year, Mindy's principal observed the teacher struggling to hold students' Attention during instruction, leading to many students failing to master critical concepts necessary for completing assignments. Many of Mindy's students appeared confused about how to complete independent work. As a result, Mindy's instructional sessions frequently deteriorated into nonproductive, sometimes contentious battles to keep her students engaged.

What made an enormous difference to Mindy was her principal's observation that she did not use Voice effectively. **He suggested that Mindy work on two techniques: (1) drop Voice to a lower register and (2) project Voice without getting overly loud.**

Mindy began by incorporating the two elements of Voice when speaking to students in non-stressful situations such as reading aloud, calling roll, or giving answers for practice tests. Gradually, Mindy became so comfortable—and increasingly skillful—with Voice that she introduced these elements into higher-stakes situations such as introducing new concepts. It seemed to Mindy that dropping her Voice to a lower register made students calmer, and projecting her Voice with appropriate tone increased students' focus. She found more students completed independent work at higher performance levels.

Example 2: Settling Unruly Students in 7th Grade Music Class

To some teachers, Stan's ability to get and maintain the Attention of groups of loud and unruly students without yelling at them seemed uncanny. When queried, Stan shared this secret with his colleagues: He initially addresses students with a Voice loud enough to carry over the noise and then gradually brings the volume down as he moves to the end of his Attention Prompt. *"I use Voice to round them up,"* Stan remarked, *"and I carefully change my voice to settle them down."* In addition, Stan uses Proximity. He pauses, looks around the room, makes eye contact with each student, and thanks them for their Attention. He then teaches his lesson or gives directions using a Voice that is pitched at a lower register, projects his words, and drops his Voice off at the ends of sentences.

Example 3: Communicating with Students Consistent with their Age Levels

Laurie Stein, a former 1st grade teacher, was struggling to relate to her 6th grade students. They sometimes mimicked her tone of Voice and her phraseology or ignored her directions. Laurie confided this problem to a colleague who had observed her with her 6th graders, and the colleague pointed to Laurie's word choices, her diction—statements like *"Now, children, let's be kind to each other," "You are such good boys and girls,"* and *"Mrs. Stein is so proud of you"*—and to the tone of her Voice, which one would expect an adult to use with primary grade students. *"Laurie, you're still talking like you did with your 1st graders. Your 6th graders don't want to be treated like babies, so they're rejecting you."*

Mrs. Stein's principal gave her a *Demo Observation Tool* and accompanied Laurie as she observed two 6th grade colleagues. Laurie made notes not only about the way these teachers framed statements to their students but also about the ways they used their Voices, which sounded respectful, businesslike and not overly sweet. Laurie used her notes to practice Voice at home and during non-stressful situations at school. She recorded her instruction and listened to her Voice tone. She worked to change her tone to sound kind but firm. Gradually, her students related to her much better and responded positively to her instruction and directions.

Recognizing Missed Opportunities for Voice

A teacher's classroom Voice is ever-present, affecting most situations that relate to students' learning. Below are four examples of situations regarding Voice. By reading left to right, you will find possible solutions for Voice failures.

Missed Opportunities for Using Classroom Voice Effectively

Classroom Situations	Voice Failure	Solution
1. Teacher presents important math concept. Students fiddle, talk, and daydream. Teacher repeats questions.	Teacher uses a loud monotone Voice that does not hold the Attention of students.	**Pitch** Voice into lower registers, projecting to reach the back row of students. Pitch Voice downward at ends of sentences.
2. Students are increasingly off task, louder and more restless as lesson progresses. Frustrated, teacher tells them they can teach themselves because they aren't listening to her.	Teacher uses a Voice from the higher, shriller ranges and speaks more loudly and rapidly as students' restlessness increases.	Teacher should first take a deep breath, **pitch** Voice to a lower register, project to students in the back. **Cadence** at the end of each sentence. Maintain a relaxed pace and **tone**.
3. Students have a pattern of becoming chatty during instruction and then quiet when teacher yells, but resume chatting moments later.	Teacher uses loud percussive Voice to quiet students but lacks Voice dynamics to hold students' Attention for long.	Pause. Make eye contact while scanning faces. Begin speaking with a calm Voice and **pitch** downward to lower register. Project Voice as needed and **cadence** at ends of sentences.
4. Middle or upper grade students appear to resent teacher speaking to them in condescending manner.	Teacher uses inappropriate tone and /or diction not suited for age levels of students.	Frame words (**diction**) in ways that respect students' ages and developmental levels. Use **tone** that conveys respect.

Consulting for Making Classroom Voice More Effective

Voice
Focused Observation Tool

Name: *Laurie Stein* Date: *11/3/09*
Grade/Subject: *6th* Observer: *J. Hite*

Elements of Voice:

Pitch: the highness or lowness of Voice (register)
Tone: the feeling conveyed by the sound of the Voice
Diction: specific word choices
Cadence: movement of Voice upward or downward

Directions: Use the following rating scale

✓ = Competent example of Voice
✓+ = Excellent example of Voice
✓– = Ineffective example at Voice

The teacher . . .

Rating	Techniques for an Effective Voice
✓	**pitches** Voice to lower register
✓	**projects** Voice to last person in the group
✓+	**drops** Voice off at the ends of sentences (**cadence**)
✓–	**maintains** Voice a comfortable pace
✓–	uses an expert **tone** of Voice to project knowledge and authority
✓	uses a developmentally appropriate **tone** of Voice for the age of her students
	chooses words (**diction**) appropriate to content and grade level

Observation Notes:

Keepers:
You kept students focused and engaged by using a voice that projected and was pitched at the lower range. Your students listened and were engaged with you.

Polishers:
When giving directions at the end of an instruction period, how might you keep your voice well modulated and at a moderate pace that keeps students engaged?

Reproducible: Page 187, Appendix

You can begin assisting teachers to develop more effective classroom Voices by collecting data about specific techniques. The *Focused Observation Tool* for Voice lists ones you can observe and rate and which your teacher can transfer and use as necessary.

Tools in this chapter will help you consult with teachers regarding the specific elements of classroom Voice. The tool on the top of this page show a principal's evaluation finding his teacher competent in four of seven Voice techniques.

This principal used the completed tool (above) for debriefing and pointed to the *Keepers*, those Voice techniques that his teacher used well, and he helped his teacher choose one or two *Polishers* for improvement. Together, they decided to address two related Voice techniques for Laurie to polish, giving her specific, achievable focal points to help her increase instructional effectiveness.

servation Tool

Name: *Laurie Stein* Date: *11/3/09*
Grade/Subject: *6th* Observer: *J. Hite*

ness or lowness of Voice (register)
g conveyed by the sound of the Voice
fic word choices
ement of Voice upward or downward
e following rating scale
etent example of Voice
ent example of Voice
tive example at Voice

	Techniques for an Effective Voice
✓	**pitches** Voice to lower register
✓	**projects** Voice to last person in the group
✓+	**drops** Voice off at the ends of sentences (**cadence**)
✓–	**maintains** Voice a comfortable pace
✓–	uses an expert **tone** of Voice to project knowledge and authority
✓	uses a developmentally appropriate **tone** of Voice for the age of her students
	chooses words (**diction**) appropriate to content and grade level

Observation Notes:

Keepers:
During formal math instruction, you kept your students focused and engaged in the lesson by using a voice that projected, yet was pitched at the lower end of the range and that dropped off at the end of each sentence. Your students could answer questions that demonstrated understanding because they were listening to and engaged with you.

Polishers:
When giving directions at the end of an instruction period, how might you keep your voice well modulated and at a moderate pace that keeps students engaged?

Consulting in Greater Depth for Voice

By using *a Depth (Interval) Observation Tool* for Voice you can collect more in-depth data for teachers who struggle with this skill. This tool lists specific purposes of using Voice on the left side of the form and the seven techniques for making Voice effective on the right. On the completed form below, Principal Long used three-minute intervals in his 30–minute observation of Ms. Woda's math class. (The most appropriate length for an interval will vary depending on the circumstances of the observation.)

Voice Depth (Interval) Observation Tool

Name: *Thereka Woda* Date: *10/3/09*
Grade/Subject: *1st* Observer: *J. Long*

Directions: For each interval you observe:

1. Place an star (★) in the box under each Voice PURPOSE and TECHNIQUE that your teacher uses effectively.
2. Put a check (✓–) under each Voice PURPOSE and TECHNIQUE that your teacher missed or didn't use effectively.
3. During your consultation, have your teacher set a goal based upon this data and the Keepers/Polishers.

	Purposes of Voice						Voice Techniques						
	Keep Students' Engagement	Calm Students/ Get Attention	Convey Information/ Directions	Project Authority and Expertise	Communicate Respect and Regard	% Engagement	Pitched at a Low Range.	Drops Off at End of Each Sentence.	Projects to Last Person in Group	Pace Comfortably	Starts Loud; Gets Lower in Volume	Appropriate Expression	Age-Appropriate Language
Interval 1		★		★	★	*85%*					★	★	
Interval 2	*✓– high, faster*		*✓–borders, shrill*	★	★	*75%*	*✓–*			*✓–*			
Interval 3	*✓– high, monotone*		*✓–high, shrill*	★	★	*70%*	*✓–*	*✓–*	*✓–*	*✓–*		★	★
Interval 4	*✓– high, monotone, louder*		*✓–high, shrill*		★	*60%*	*✓–*	*✓–*	*✓–*	*✓–*			★
Interval 5	*✓– high, monotone, louder, faster*		*✓–high, shrill*			*50%*	*✓–*	*✓–*	*✓–*	*✓–*			*✓–*
Interval 6	*✓– high, monotone, louder, faster*		*✓–high, shrill*		*✓– frustration*	*35%*	*✓–*	*✓–*	*✓–*	*✓–*			*✓–*
Interval 7		★ *deep breath, Attention*			*✓–sarcasm, frustration*	*75%*					★		★
Interval 8	★		★	★	★	*85%*	★	★	★	★			★
Interval 9	*✓– high, faster*		*✓– shrill*			*72%*	*✓–*			*✓–*			
Interval 10	*✓– high, monotone*		*✓– high, shrill*	★	★	*60%*	*✓–*	*✓–*	*✓–*	*✓–*		★	★

Keepers: *Your use of Voice at the beginnings of your instruction is extremely effective. Students appear calm and focused. Real learning takes place.*

Polishers: *Use strategies for holding students' attentions during longer periods of instruction.*

Teacher Goal: *I will focus on using my voice to keep students engaged. Two techniques I will concentrate on using are (1) speaking in the lower voice registers and (2) dropping my voice off at the end of each sentence.*

Reproducible: Page 188, Appendix

As you examine the *Interval Observation Tool,* notice the pattern that the data reflects. Ms. Woda uses her Voice effectively to calm students and get their Attention, initially achieving 85% engagement. However, when she instructs for any sustained period, she fails to use Voice techniques that keep students engaged. From Intervals 1 through 4 (12 minutes), student engagement gradually drops from 85% to 60%. Notice that during those Intervals her Voice rises, shriller and louder. Problems accelerate through Intervals 5 and 6 as Ms. Woda talks for 6 minutes in a loud monotonous Voice culminating in sarcasm. Student engagement plummets to 35%. At Interval 7, Ms. Woda pauses, takes a deep breath, and then asks for students' Attention using appropriate Voice techniques. She continues to use effective Voice techniques to keep students engaged for three minutes during Interval 8. In Intervals 9 and 10, she gradually begins to lose the Voice focus and a pattern of disengagement begins again.

During his post-observation consultation, Principal Coates used this data to help Ms. Woda identify and discuss the patterns it revealed. He helped her see that she does use her Voice effectively to calm students and to get their Attention, but she struggles to sustain engagement. The principal assisted Ms. Woda to set a goal to improve two Voice techniques: First, to speak in the lower Voice **register** that is more comfortable for students to listen to, and second, to **cadence** at the ends of sentences.

Other Strategies for Consulting about Voice

Another way administrators can help teachers develop effective classroom Voice is by guiding them through a focused observation of another teacher.

Guide Your Teacher through a Demo Observation. A demo observation provides your teacher with an opportunity to observe one to two teachers who skillfully employ Voice techniques to keep their students engaged. Using this simple *Demo Observation Tool* for Voice, teachers can (1) identify specific elements of an effective classroom Voice, (2) describe briefly each element that the teacher uses well, and (3) make note of students' responses for each interval.

During your debriefing, ask your teacher to describe effective uses of the demonstration teacher's Voice—pitch, tone, diction, cadence—as well as the resulting effects on students' Attention and behavior. Then help your teacher set one or two goals for specific techniques to incorporate into his or her own classroom Voice.

To the right is an example of a *Demo Observation Tool* for Voice that Al Lowman completed during a session observing Ms. Peas, the demonstration teacher.

Voice Demo Observation Tool

Observer: *Al Lowman* Grade/Class: *4th self-contained*
Demo Teacher: *Serenity Peas* Date/Time: *10/23/09*

Elements of Voice: Voice can be analyzed for Pitch (highness, lowness), Tone (attitude), Diction (word choices), and Cadence (modulation).

Directions: Describe actions by your demonstration teacher that reveal elements of his or her Voice, and enter these descriptions in the center column. Then, for each description, enter your perception of the Voice in the left column, and describe students' responses to those actions and Voice in the right column.

Voice Purpose	Teacher Action (Uses of Voice)	Student Response
Calm students	*Students returned from recess more raucously than usual. Ms. Peas signaled for attention in a voice loud enough for all to hear, then gradually decreased the volume and slowed the pace of her voice.*	*Students were initially noisy and a bit rowdy. They turned toward Ms. Peas and had completely quieted down and given her their attention by the end of the signal.*
Keep students engaged	*When a few students began having side conversations, Ms. Peas lowered her voice to a lower register then dropped it off at the end of each sentence. Her voice projected to the back row of students.*	*Students quit talking, leaned forward, and listened more attentively.*
Convey information and give directions	*During math instruction, Ms. Peas spoke to students in a voice with a relaxed pace in a low voice range that was comfortable for students to listen to, yet conveyed energy.*	*Students were relaxed and attentive to Ms. Peas's instruction. 95% of students responded to her engagement prompts. Students' answers to questions showed understanding.*
Communicate authority and expertise	*During instruction, Ms. Peas spoke in an expert voice that conveyed confidence and authority.*	*90% of students completely attended to her lesson, confident that they could learn something from her.*
Communicate respect and regard	*1. Ms. Peas redirected two students who were fiddling in a quiet, calm voice that only they could hear.* *2. Ms. Peas, who had been a 1st grade teacher, used language with students that communicated that they had maturity and capability.*	*1. The two students stopped fiddling and returned to their work in a cooperative manner.* *2. Students seemed to feel pride in their ability to function well in class.*

Teacher Transfer: In my classroom, I want to:
Transferring the ability to use my voice to calm rowdy students down without yelling at them. To do so, at the first of my request for attention, I will use a voice loud enough for all to hear and then gradually bring the volume down while still projecting my voice throughout the class.

Reproducible: Page 189, Appendix

Shadow Your Teacher for an Effective Classroom Voice. Here's a sports analogy: Shadowing is similar to positioning your child, a beginning skier, between your knees while you whisper directions to train your child to execute specific moves. By shadowing, you help your teacher (1) recognize opportunities and select the right Voice techniques at the right time, (2) use Voice to increase student engagement, (3) keep students calm, and (4) project authority/expertise—even help build a teacher-student relationship of respect and regard.

To shadow in close Proximity to your teacher, cross behind as needed to whisper suggestions to use Voice for a particular purpose or to use a specific Voice technique to capture and sustain students' attention. A less invasive form of shadowing is to Signal the teacher from the side of the room. To use this approach, you two need to identify specific Signals you will use to alert the teacher to use Voice for a a variety of purposes. For instance, if students are losing focus and your teacher needs to pitch Voice to a lower register, you might point your index finger down. If, on the other hand, the Voice is low but monotonous, you might use your fingers to indicate a downward motion to identify cadence—dropping Voice at the ends of sentences.

Here are some Signals you might use during a shadowing event.

Indicators for Shadowing Voice Techniques

Desired Voice Technique	Indicator
Pitch Voice to a low range.	Point index finger down.
Project to last person in the group.	Point to the back row of students.
Cadence at the ends of sentences.	Scribe downward motion in the air.
Keep Voice at a comfortable pace.	Walk fingers up your arms fast or slowly, to show if pace needs to adjust slower or faster.
Start loud enough to project over noise. Gradually quiet and use an Attention Prompt to calm students.	Make a > with your hands to connote starting with a loud voice and gradually becoming more quiet.
Soften Voice so as not to compete with the ideas being presented.	Cup your hand by your ear.
Project expertise and authority.	Square your shoulders and hold your head up high.
Tailor Voice to the age of students.	Give a thumbs-up.
Make diction appropriate to age of students.	Make circular motions with your hand by your mouth and smile.

Consider Using a System of Stickers and Tape. The teacher places a strip of tape on a clipboard to carry during instruction. For each use of Voice to accomplish one particular purpose, the teacher places a sticker on the tape strip for the technique used effectively. For example, if a teacher consciously uses Voice to keep students engaged, she would put four stickers, one each for pitching Voice in a lower register, dropping it at the end of each sentence, projecting it to the back of the room, and pacing at an appropriate speed.

Try Audio/Video Recording. You may find this a fruitful technique. To change one's Voice, one must first hear it as others do. Have your teacher record instruction for a 10– to 15–minute time period and then listen for one of the Voice elements. Afterwards, your teacher can practice using a different register and/or volume level. Video recording may also be helpful for the teacher to see the impact of voice on student behavior.

Coaching for an Effective Classroom Voice

One of the desired outcomes of coaching is for teachers to use self-reflection in refining areas of their practice. The coaching process consists of a pre-conference to plan for the observation, the observation itself, and the post-conference to reflect on the data and to make refinement goals.

During pre-conferences, your role as coach is to help your teachers think through lessons to anticipate situations that call for them to use Voices in certain ways to accomplish specific purposes and to identify Voice techniques they think they need to employ. For example, if the observation were to take place during physical education, the teacher may anticipate using Voice to get students' Attention during a game. Once the purpose was identified, the teacher would select the relevant technique of starting the Signal with a Voice loud enough that most students will hear it and then gradually bring down the volume. This technique nearly always calms students and prepares them for listening. As you help your teacher think through the lesson, help identify other purposes for using Voice effectively. Together, you and your teacher should select or design an observation instrument for collecting Voice data.

Following are some questions you could use to facilitate your teacher's thinking.

Coaching Conversation for Voice
Questions for Planning a Visit and Observation

- What is your Voice goal during your lesson?
- Walk me through your lesson.
  - List the points in your lesson in which you will need to be mindful of your Voice goal for this lesson?
  - What techniques will you have to be conscious of incorporating in your Voice?
- What behavioral problems do you foresee? How can you use your Voice to preempt these problems from occurring?
- What will you see (e.g., student behaviors) that will Cue you to refocus the use of your Voice?
- How will you know if you are using an effective Voice?

During the post-observation conference with your data, you and your teacher will note patterns, strengths, and areas to refine. At the conclusion of the conference, help your teacher set a goal and move forward in developing an effective classroom Voice. Select a date for the next coaching cycle. Here are some possible questions you could use during the post-conference.

Reflective Conversation Questions Following the Visit and Observation

- How did it go? Did you meet your goal for Voice? How do you know?
- Did your plans to use Voice go as planned? Why or why not?
- What patterns do you see in the data I shared with you?
- What does this data tell you about your classroom Voice?
- What did you learn about the use of your Voice that you want to replicate every time you teach?
- What ONE thing do you want to refine to enhance your classroom Voice?

12
The Process in Context

The standards you found in Chapter 1 represent one district's decisions and hard work distilling multiple sources of insight into the parts or domains that contribute to the Whole Picture of instruction and learning. Utah's Granite School District identified Four Domains of Instruction and Learning to represent their official educational standards. Specific aspects of these domains became the benchmarks for formal and informal observations made by every building administrator in the district and, like many other districts, were derived from the work of experts like Charlotte Danielsen and the *Framework for Instruction* (Danielson, 1996; Danielson & McGreal, 2000).

Like Granite, some other districts also identify Four Domains while others may identify Five. As you know, each domain focuses on specific elements of teaching practice, but all domains work together to provide a complete picture of effective teaching practices that contribute to high quality student learning. **Teachers set goals and design instruction (Domain I) by creating and managing an environment of respectful, coherent instruction (Domain II) and engage students at high levels of positive learning (Domain III) while growing professionally and embracing promising new instructional practices (Domain IV). And whether your district presents its standards across four or five domains, in all likelihood your district's standards have been influenced by earlier models, propositions, and standards that for decades have been shaping the way educators look at students and their learning.**

Also influential upon the development of educator guidelines is the *National Board for Professional Teaching Standards* (NBPTS), an "independent, nonprofit, nonpartisan and nongovernmental organization...formed in 1987 to advance the quality of teaching and learning by developing professional standards for accomplished teaching." NBPTS sets forth its vision for instruction and learning in Five Core Propositions to "form the foundation and frame the rich amalgam of knowledge, skills, dispositions, and beliefs that characterize National Board Certified Teachers (NBCTs)."

Proposition 1: Teachers are Committed to Students and Their Learning.

Proposition 2: Teachers Know the Subjects They Teach and How to Teach Those Subjects to Students.

Proposition 3: Teachers are Responsible for Managing and Monitoring Student Learning.

Proposition 4: Teachers Think Systematically about Their Practice and Learn from Experience.

Proposition 5: Teachers are Members of Learning Communities.

If you decide to introduce your process for observations and assistance by placing it into a broad context, you might begin by focusing on national standards—such as those presented here in this chapter or in Chapter 2—or else you can focus specifically on your own district's. Surely, you and your staff can find much to talk about, particularly if discussion begins with a focus on successes past and present.

Place Your Process in Context

A discussion about educator standards easily leads to most teachers' immediate interests—the student and the classroom experience—and as you find in so many formal outlines of educator standards, that means Domain III (for districts like Granite) or Proposition 3 (for NCBTs). Teaching standards are the foundation around which your supervisory process is built, and they are the underpinning of your teachers' practices.

Ethically, administrators have an obligation to introduce, explain, and discuss district standards with teachers before expecting them to demonstrate proficiency in meeting them. Once you have presented or offered hard copies of your district's standards to your teachers, we recommend that you move toward discussions with your staff to focus on The Big Eight engagement strategies herein: Expectations, Attention Prompts, Proximity, Cueing, Signals, Time Limits, Tasking, and Voice. These engagement skills directly address your standards, just as they address Domain III in Granite's Teaching Standards; and they encompass key classroom management skills that, when used effectively, will significantly increase student engagement and therefore learning.

Present Your Process to Your Staff

For an administrator, a key element of establishing a system of observing and evaluating teachers is sharing the larger picture with them or, to put it another way, inviting teachers into the full context of what you seek to achieve. As you know, professionals of all types are much more able and willing to respond to specific criteria and Expectations if they have clear understandings of what those specific Expectations are. Since much of your work with your teachers will focus on their classroom management skills, you might start early in the year to disclose your basic observation criteria, including The Big Eight, and to provide general statements about your wishes for their success. Emphasize that your relationship with each of your teachers as well as each of their relationships with each other will be key elements—indeed, they will be the critical synergies—for the real growth everyone desires in the year ahead.

The purpose we have developed for you fits into the greater needs of your school in two very important ways. First, it pursues the goal that every student will make at least a year's academic growth, and second, it provides you and your teachers with tools and technical support for engagement to help each and every one increase instructional capabilities and enhance effectiveness.

Presenting an overview of your supervisory process to your staff will only further your goals and can encourage your teachers to begin focusing on their strengths and their skills, and to continue thinking about the possibilities for growth before them.

Treat this chapter as an outline you might use to prepare your staff for participating in this growth-promoting process with you. Lay down the foundation by introducing the major components of your supervisory stances (observer, consultant, coach, etc.), share the tools you will use, and clarify your function or your purpose: to sharpen teachers' instructional skills by enhancing their performance and professional satisfaction in order to increase student learning.

Consider using a two-pronged approach once you have placed your district's standards into the context of growth: First, introduce the tools you will use (*Drop-Ins, Time-on-Tasks*, etc.) and any others you wish. Second, review the *Time-on-Task Tool* closely so that you can clarify The Big Eight, particularly for new or struggling teachers. If you pace your approach over three or four meetings, you might focus on the following topics in the sequence outlined in the next chart.

Introducing Your Observation Engagement Process to Teachers

Topic for Staff Discussion	Possible Meeting Format	Audience
Administrator Stances: Evaluator, consultant, coach, collaborator	Faculty Meeting—30 to 45 minutes	All Teachers
The Big 8 Engagement Skills: Expectations, Attention Prompts, Proximity, Cueing, Signals, Time Limits, Tasking, and Voice	Faculty Meeting—30 to 45 minutes	All Teachers
Drop-Ins	Faculty Meeting—15 to 20 minutes	All Teachers
Time-on-Task Tool	Small Group Meeting: Teams or Individuals	New Teachers Struggling Teachers

Know and Explain Your Stances

As you saw in Chapter 2, your choice of stance is one of your most critical decisions because knowing your stance helps you guide the observations, debriefings, and other strategies in your work with each teacher. Introducing and describing the stances that you will employ can be as simple as providing simple definitions for your teachers, yet this bit of clarity may go a long way toward focusing and facilitating your working relationships with each of them. Here are your stances in a nutshell: This next little chart might, in itself, help you focus a 30– to 45–minute staff discussion.

Stances for Observing and Assisting	
My Stance	**My Role**
Evaluate	To Dictate
Consult	To Tell and Show
Coach	To Ask
Collaborate	To Share

Keep in mind that nearly every professional at one time or another has wished for a benevolent coach, a consultant, a collaborator—someone on their side. These purposes and tools and these skills and strategies, however you tweak them or make them your own, can help you reach out to your teachers constructively and collaboratively.

Share The Big Eight Engagement Skills

These terms will not feel like rocket science to your teachers. Quite the contrary, they probably will seem obvious, common sense.

One simple way to introduce The Big Eight is to share with teachers the chart you found in Chapter 2. Here is a version you will find as a reproducible in the Appendix.

One activity you might try with your teachers is first to provide each with a copy of The Big Eight and then to ask them to read each skill term and definition. Invite them to do the following silently:

- Place an "N" by the skills that they do naturally, unconsciously.
- Place a ✓ by one or two skills that they may most want to focus on consciously—that is, the ones that they think they can sharpen in ways that might impact student engagement.

Ask teachers to share their N's and ✓'s with a partner. You might point out that gathering data on these skills can further inform their professional development goals throughout the school year. You might ask a volunteer or two to share and discuss their N's and ✓'s, or you might wait for your next one-on-one meetings. Use your judgment.

The Big Eight Engagement Skills for Instruction		
1	**Expectations**	Teacher ensures that students know what to do and when and how to do it.
2	**Attention Prompts**	Teacher uses verbal or visual prompts to focus students' attention for instruction to follow.
3	**Proximity**	Teacher moves purposefully around the classroom for maximum effect.
4	**Cueing**	Teacher uses positive, clear and effective verbal Cues to clarify, maintain, or redirect activity.
5	**Signals**	Teacher uses nonverbal Signals to direct performance, student responses, and other activity.
6	**Time Limits**	Teacher identifies and communicates specific times for beginning and completing tasks.
7	**Tasking**	Teacher focuses and sharpens students' engagement through questioning strategies, purposeful and thought-provoking activities, and other tactics to direct their learning.
8	**Voice**	Teacher uses Voice to maximum effect: pitch in the lower registers, tone geared for situations, diction appropriate to students' age levels, and voice modulation, or cadence, to maintain interest.

Reproducible: Page 190, Appendix

Clarify the Nature and Purpose of Drop-Ins

Generally, teachers respect and appreciate brief visits, or *Drop-Ins*. Many appreciate feedback such as the *Keepers* and *Polishers* you can supply. Most teachers recognize advantages and benefits from having an administrator who is aware of what is going on in day-to-day classroom learning and who can offer ideas, support, and assistance.

Be sure that your teachers understand the concept and purpose of *Drop-Ins:* These are short visits that focus on physical environment and general learning environment. The latter, the learning environment, is enhanced by The Big Eight. Some administrators use meeting times early in the year to explain the concept and purpose of *Drop-Ins*, making references to them as needed during subsequent faculty meetings.

To help your teachers become familiar with *Drop-Ins*, you might take these simple steps:

- Provide each teacher with a blank ***Drop-In Tool*** and a blank ***Reflection Follow-Up*** card.
- Ask teachers to highlight one or two skill areas (on Part B of the *Drop-In Tool* under "Classroom Management Environment") that they are trying to improve in their daily teaching for the purpose of increasing levels of student engagement.
- Then, on the bottom of the *Drop-In*, ask teachers to write a *Keeper* (something they feel they do especially well for student engagement) and a *Polisher* (a skill or strategy they would most like to improve). Ask teachers to copy the *Keeper* and *Polisher* onto the *Reflection Follow-Up* card, and explain that your practice will be to keep the *Drop-In Tool* but leave behind the card.
- Ask teachers to pass these completed *Reflection Follow-Up* cards to you. Tell your staff that you will read these carefully and will focus on the information during your *Drop-Ins.*
- You might identify a Signal that your teachers can use to let you know that a *Drop-In* might not be a good idea at that time, or you can ask teachers to suggest a Signal to you. (Note to self: If a teacher Signals you more than two times in a row, consider it an alert that this teacher may be struggling more than most with classroom management.)
- Always emphasize to your teachers that you welcome individual conversations with them including feedback regarding their *Reflection Follow-Up* cards.

Explain the *Time-on-Task Tool*

Early in the year, you may decide to show and demonstrate *only* the *Drop-In Tool*. If you decide to discuss others, here are some major points to cover.

- ***Time-on-Task Tool*** helps collect data about specific engagement skills to expedite growth celebrate and success. You might point out the helpfulness of using this tool with new teachers and those who express interest or need in focusing on specific engagement skills. For new teachers, the information from this tool can take months off the learning curve.
- ***Focused Observation*** and ***Depth Observation Tools*** can yield still more data about specific engagement skills. These tools help analyze a teacher's progress and provide insight into tactics and strategies that are working as well as those needing to be sharpened.
- ***Demo Observation Tool*** helps some teachers identify specific tactics and strategies used by other teachers to achieve high levels of student engagement.

Invite Your Teachers To Make Student Engagement a Priority

Why focus on engagement skills and strategies? *It's where the rubber meets the road.* This seems undeniably true, as **there can be no greater goal than to increase engagement to improve learning.**

Most of your teachers—possibly all of them—can recall courses they took on educational theory and lesson planning, but few—possibly none of them—can recall specific, hands-on guidance they received about *managing* lessons and about facilitating student engagement in learning. Such a deficiency is unfortunate as it provides no running start for new teachers, meaning that only the most naturally gifted can fly high at the outset.

The good news is that *you*, the administrator-observer-consultant-coach, can provide that leg up for your new teachers, your struggling ones, your mature-experienced and young-progressive teachers, and even your wise veterans. Everyone can benefit. You can do this by focusing on engagement *early* in the year and by reprising this theme regularly *during* the year—with some or all of your teachers. You may see benefits quickly as you experience fewer office referrals and parental complaints and find you're putting out fewer fires. Best of all, you will have set into motion a capacity-building process for your teachers—one that regenerates—the results of which will lead to more students learning at higher levels.

And then, once you've digested the trite but sunny clichés on this page (you noticed them, right? *rubber meets the road, running start, flying high, reprising a theme, putting out fires)* you can make this process *entirely your own.* **It really doesn't matter if you choose to redefine The Big Eight or if you alter the tools or invent new ones. It doesn't matter. What's important is that you and your teachers think actively about student engagement and about the techniques that might work best. Integrate engagement into your observation and consultation process. And good luck!**

Appendix

Tools for Observation and Direct Assistance

Domain III: Standards and Rubric for Learning Environment

Standard	ABOVE STANDARD (3)	MEETS STANDARD (2)	APPROACHES STANDARD (1)	BELOW STANDARD (0)	SCORE
LEARNING ENVIRONMENT—DOMAIN III					
A. The educator shows and elicits respect while developing and maintaining positive rapport.	• Fosters a safe/ equitable learning community. • Facilitates student participation in creating a climate of equity and respect.	• Facilitates a caring and motivating environment. • Encourages positive social interaction. • Promotes cooperative and collaborative learning.	• Builds rapport with most students. • Models respectful relationships. • Utilizes some strategies to respond to disrespect.	• Disrespect is exhibited by teacher and students. • Rules are inconsistent.	
B. The educator advocates, nurtures, and sustains a culture for learning.	• Encourages students to set personal goals and high expectations. • Designs movement patterns and access to resources to promote engagement.	• Sets and maintains high expectations. • Develops self-motivation and active engagement in learning. • Recognizes the importance of establishing a climate of learning.	• Develops some expectations. • Applies engagement strategies. • Provides opportunities for group interaction.	• Inconsistent or low Expectations. • No Expectations for students to engage in their own learning or to work with peers.	
C. The educator manages procedures.	• Assists all students in developing and internalizing equitable routines, procedures, and habits. • Facilitates student ownership of classroom habits and procedures.	• Arranges and directs procedures with minimum disruption. • Manages transitions effectively. • Maximizes the amount of time spent in learning. • Applies procedures and enforces rules consistently.	• Establishes some procedures and classroom rules to support student learning. • Develops student awareness of the procedures. • Spends the majority of structured time learning (e.g., reading, content focus).	• Minimal or no classroom rules or procedures are evident. • Teacher directions and procedures are confusing. • Instructional time is lost during transitions.	
D. The educator manages student behavior.	• Presents, adjusts, and facilitates instruction and daily activities so students are engaged. • Facilitates student problem solving of interpersonal conflicts.	• Explains rules, expectations, and consequences. • Explains reasons for disciplinary actions. • Administers discipline that fits the infraction in a calm, professional demeanor. • Uses fair and consistent practices.	• Communicates rules and consequences. • Responds to disruptive behavior. • Develops some routines for classroom procedures.	• Rules are not defined or communicated to students. • Discipline is inconsistent and does not correlate to the infraction.	
E. The educator prepares and maintains an environment conducive to learning	• Uses the physical environment to promote individual and group learning.	• Designs movement and resources to promote individual and group engagement. • Uses room displays in learning activities.	• Manages room for easy movement and access to resources. • Uses room displays that represent current topics of study.	• Movement patterns are awkward.	

Drop-In Tool

Name: ______________________ Date/Time: ______________

Grade/Subject: ________________ Observer: ______________

Rating System:

✓+ = Strategy exceptionally well done ✓– = Strategy attempted, not effective

✓ = Strategy apparent and competent – = Strategy missing, should occur

Physical Environment: (Domain III. Learning Environment):

___ Student work is on display and clearly demonstrates the objective

___ Student Expectations for behavior are posted

___ Room is organized with easy access to materials

___ Room arrangement lends itself to physical movement

___ Learning objective is posted

___ Schedule is posted

Classroom Management/Engagement: (Domain III. Learning Environment):

___ Students know what to do and when and how to do it (EXPECTATIONS)

___ Teacher uses prompts to focus instruction to follow (ATTENTION)

___ Teacher moves purposefully around the classroom (PROXIMITY)

___ Teacher uses positive, effective verbal Cues (CUEING)

___ Teacher uses nonverbal Signals to direct students (SIGNALS)

___ Teacher offers times for beginning and ending tasks (TIME LIMITS)

___ Teacher sharpens engagement through questioning strategies (TASKING)

___ Teacher uses positive, clear, effective tone and verbiage (VOICE)

Student Engagement: (Domain III. Learning Environment): 25 # students

Approximate PERCENTAGE of student engagement: ________

Students are engaged in work directly related to the objective. ____ YES ____ NO

Comments/Questions: ____

____

____

Follow-Up: ____

____

____

Reflection Follow-Up

Name: ______________________ Date: __________

Grade/Subject: ______________ Observer: ____________

Keepers: ____________________________________

____

____

____

____

Polishers: ____________________________________

____

____

____

____

Reflection Follow-Up

Name: ______________________ Date: __________

Grade/Subject: ______________ Observer: ____________

Keepers: ____________________________________

____

____

____

____

Polishers: ____________________________________

____

____

____

____

Time-On-Task (Observation Tool for All Engagement Skills)

Name: ______________ Date: ______________ # Students: ________ Grade/Class: ______________ Observer: ______________

Directions: Record the time for each observation you make of educator involvement in learning. Record observations as follows:

1. Mark percentage of student engagement. (P) passive, (A) active
2. Describe teacher actions causing disengagement.
3. Describe relevant student behavior, especially off-task behavior.
4. Ask yourself, "What would I do if I were the teacher?"
5. Check recommended action(s)—those things that you would do if you were the teacher. You may also want to ★ actions that the teacher performs well.

FOR EACH INTERVAL, show % of Student Engagement.

WRITE **A** for alert, attentive behavior, or
P for passive, disengaged behavior. **THEN DESCRIBE**

INTERVALS	Teacher Actions Impacting Students (Below) AND	Student Engagement and Behavior (Below)	Expectations	Attention Prompts	Proximity	Cueing	Signals	Time Limits	Tasking	Voice
			RECOMMENDED ACTIONS							
Interval No. 1 ________ ________	% Engaged: ____ 0–5% ____ 6–25% ____ 26–33%	____ 34–50% ____ 51–79% ____ 80–100%								
	Teacher Actions:	**Student Behavior:**								
Interval No. 2 ________ ________	% Engaged: ____ 0–5% ____ 6–25% ____ 26–33%	____ 34–50% ____ 51–79% ____ 80–100%								
	Teacher Actions:	**Student Behavior:**								
Interval No. 3 ________ ________	% Engaged: ____ 0–5% ____ 6–25% ____ 26–33%	____ 34–50% ____ 51–79% ____ 80–100%								
	Teacher Actions:	**Student Behavior:**								
Interval No. 4 ________ ________	% Engaged: ____ 0–5% ____ 6–25% ____ 26–33%	____ 34–50% ____ 51–79% ____ 80–100%								
	Teacher Actions:	**Student Behavior:**								
Interval No. 5 ________ ________	% Engaged: ____ 0–5% ____ 6–25% ____ 26–33%	____ 34–50% ____ 51–79% ____ 80–100%								
	Teacher Actions:	**Student Behavior:**								

Recommended Actions:

Teacher Action/ Student Response Tool

Name: ______________________ Date: __________

Grade/Subject: ______________ Observer: ______________

Use For:	Directions:
♦ Nonverbal Feedback: body language, gestures, proximity, eye contact ♦ Responding to difficult students ♦ Effectiveness of teacher directions	1. Write the time. Attempt 1- to 3-minute intervals. 2. Write the teacher action that he/she has asked you to collect data (directions, praise, nonverbal cues, etc). 3. Write the student response. 4. Write approximate percentage of students that are on task.

Time	Teacher Action	Student(s) Response	%

Differentiation Observation Tool

Name: ____________________ Date: ____________

Grade/Subject: ____________ Observer: ____________

Use For:

- Differentiation (Curriculum Based) Observation
- How are the needs of each level of learner being met?

Directions:

Collect teacher action and student response in relation to each level of learners.
(It may be helpful to have a class chart that identifies levels of students for the observation.)

	Below Level		Average		Above Average	
Objective	Teacher Action	Student Response	Teacher Action	Student Response	Teacher Action	Student Response

Questioning Observation Tool

Name: __________ Date: __________

Grade/Subject: __________ Observer: __________

Directions:

1. Script teacher's questions/directions for response in the appropriate column.
2. During debriefing, coach the teacher to adjust verbiage to move into engagement column.

Assessment (Average 5% response) One student/one response. Raising of hand—calling on one child. e.g., *"Deyanne, who are the main characters?"*	**Open (Average 30% to 40% response)** "Fishing" for an answer. Students don't know how to respond. Question asked usually with no wait time—whoever wants to answer responds, e.g., *"Who are the main characters?"*	**Engagement (Average 90% response)** 1. Response method given before the question. *"Show me (finger count) how many characters are in the story." "Whisper to your neighbor the main characters in the story."* 2. Physical Cue to raise hand or chorally respond.

Cooperative Learning Observation Tool

Name: ______________________ Date: __________

Grade/Subject: ______________ Observer: ____________

Directions:

1. Observe the entire cooperative learning event in order to collect behavioral and academic data.
2. For each category, write down the teacher's verbiage and the students' response (physical and academic).

Time	Cooperative Learning	Student Response
	Academic Task:	
	Criteria for Success:	
	Group Interdependence:	
	Individual Accountability:	
	Expected Behaviors:	
	Need for Behavior:	
	Define the Behavior:	
	Practice the Behavior:	
	Evaluation:	

Lesson Sequence Observation Tool

Name: ______________________ Date: __________

Grade/Subject: ______________ Observer: ______________

Use For:	Directions:
Lesson Sequence (direct instruction/ guided practice/independent practice)	1. Observe during a direct instruction lesson. 2. Collect teacher action and student response for each part of the lesson.

Time	Lesson Sequence	Student Response
	Objective	
	Direct Instruction	
	Assessment	
	Guided Practice	
	Assessment	
	Independent Practice	
	Assessment	

Engagement VS Individual Student(s) Tool

Name: ______________ Date: ______________

Grade/Subject: ______________ Observer: ______________

Instructions (Remember to not worry about FFAASSTT Intervals).

1. Write the time.
2. Circle the percentage of engaged students (and if appropriate X the percentage of quiet students/R the percentage of responding (verbally and/or kinesthetically) students.
3. Write what you see students doing
4. Write (specifically) what student A and student B are doing.

Time	Class Engagement	Student A	Student B
Interval 1	5 10 15 20 25 30 35 40 45 50 55 60 65 70 75 80 85 90 95 100		
Interval 2	5 10 15 20 25 30 35 40 45 50 55 60 65 70 75 80 85 90 95 100		
Interval 3	5 10 15 20 25 30 35 40 45 50 55 60 65 70 75 80 85 90 95 100		
Interval 4	5 10 15 20 25 30 35 40 45 50 55 60 65 70 75 80 85 90 95 100		
Interval 5	5 10 15 20 25 30 35 40 45 50 55 60 65 70 75 80 85 90 95 100		
Interval 6	5 10 15 20 25 30 35 40 45 50 55 60 65 70 75 80 85 90 95 100		
Interval 7	5 10 15 20 25 30 35 40 45 50 55 60 65 70 75 80 85 90 95 100		
Interval 8	5 10 15 20 25 30 35 40 45 50 55 60 65 70 75 80 85 90 95 100		
Interval 9	5 10 15 20 25 30 35 40 45 50 55 60 65 70 75 80 85 90 95 100		
Interval 10	5 10 15 20 25 30 35 40 45 50 55 60 65 70 75 80 85 90 95 100		
Interval 11	5 10 15 20 25 30 35 40 45 50 55 60 65 70 75 80 85 90 95 100		

Expectations Focused Observation Tool

Name: ______________________ Date: ______________

Grade/Subject: ______________ Observer: ______________

Directions: Observe student behaviors and procedures as they reflect teacher's Expectations.

✓ = Competent example of Expectations
✓+ = Excellent example of Expectations
✓− = Ineffective attempt of Expectations

The teacher . . .

	communicates immediate Expectations clearly
	communicates clear Expectations for simple procedures such as giving and getting Attention, entering the classroom, self-starting, moving within classroom, etc.
	communicates clear Expectations for complex procedures such as participating in learning centers, using math manipulatives, partner reading, cooperative learning

Observation Notes:

Keepers:

____

____

____

____

____

Polishers:

____

____

____

____

____

Expectations Depth Observation Tool

Name: ______________________ Date: __________

Grade/Subject: ______________ Observer: __________

Directions: Describe student behaviors and procedures as they reflect teacher's Expectations and note missed opportunities

Expectations that are Established	Expectations that are Reinforced	Missed Opportunities

Observation Notes:

Keepers:

____

____

____

____

Polishers:

____

____

____

____

Expectations Demo Observation Tool

Observer: ____________ Grade/Class: ____________

Demo Teacher: ____________ Date/Time: ____________

Directions: Describe specific student behaviors and procedures as they reflect teacher's Expectations. Then set a goal for transferring a strategy into instruction of your own

Immediate Expectations (Short Term)		Habitual Expectations (Long Term)	
Teacher Action	**Student Response**	**Teacher Action**	**Student Response**

Teacher Transfer: In my classroom, I want to set and refine this Expectation:

Attention Prompts Focused Observation Tool

Name: ______________________ Date: __________

Grade/Subject: ______________ Observer: __________

Directions: Observe student behaviors and procedures as they reflect teacher's Expectations.

✓ = Competent example of Attention Prompts
✓+ = Excellent example of Attention Prompts
✓– = Ineffective attempt of Attention Prompts

The teacher . . .

	gives student a warning that an Attention Prompt is coming
	uses an Attention Prompt before instructing
	is in the teacher position and ready to instruct
	uses a credible voice
	Prompt Steps ____ prompts ____ pauses for 2 to 3 seconds making eye contact ____ gives two positive Cues ____ begins teaching immediately

Observation Notes:

Keepers:

____

____

____

____

____

Polishers:

____

____

____

____

____

Attention Prompts Demo Observation Tool

Observer: ______________________ Grade/Class: ____________________

Demo Teacher: ______________________ Date/Time: ______________

Directions: Describe specific Attention Prompts as they reflect teacher's Expectations, and describe specific student responses to those prompts.

Prompt		Pause Making Eye Contact		Positive Cues	
Teacher Action	**Student Response**	**Teacher Action**	**Student Response**	**Teacher Action**	**Student Response**

Teacher Transfer: In my classroom, I want to set and refine this use of Attention:

Proximity
Focused Observation Tool

Name: ______________________ Date: __________

Grade/Subject: ______________ Observer: __________

Directions: Observing for Physical Positioning, Visual Scanning, and Presence.

✓ = Competent example of Proximity

✓+ = Excellent example of Proximity

✓– = Ineffective attempt of Proximity

The teacher . . .

	moves throughout the classroom while instructing (physical positioning)
	moves throughout the classroom during independent practice (physical positioning)
	maintains eye contact with students (visual scanning)
	achieves Proximity between small groups (physical positioning)
	communicates authority nonverbally (presence)

Observation Notes:

Keepers:

____

____

____

____

____

Polishers:

____

____

____

____

____

Proximity Spatial Observation Tool

Name: ______________________ Date: __________

Grade/Subject: ______________ Observer: __________

Teacher Movement/Student Participation **Cooperative Learning/Centers**

Use For:	**Directions:**
♦ Monitoring student progress and independent work ♦ Time spent with each group ♦ Teacher movement throughout the classroom ♦ On-task behavior ♦ Proximity	1. Track the time and percentage of on-task students in 3–5 min intervals. 2. Using this chart as a map of the classroom, track the teacher's movement by placing a dot showing the teacher's physicality. Each time the teacher moves, put another dot. It is helpful to note the time by each dot. 3. Mark in the boxes (tables) a '+' to show on-task behavior and a '–' to show off-task behavior for each student in 3-5 minute intervals.

Time	%

Proximity Demo Observation Tool

Observer: ______________________ Grade/Class: ________________

Demo Teacher: ______________________ Date/Time: ______________

Directions: Describe specific uses of Proximity in three areas (Physical Positioning, Visual Scanning, and Presence), and describe student behavior that results from each use of Proximity.

Physical Positioning Location in the room		**Visual Scanning** Eye-to-eye Contact		**Presence** Posture/Poise	
Teacher Action	**Student Response**	**Teacher Action**	**Student Response**	**Teacher Action**	**Student Response**

Teacher Transfer: In my classroom, I want to focus on:

Teacher Movement Student Participation

Name: ____________________ Date: ____________

Grade/Subject: ____________________ Observer: ____________________

Use For:

- Monitoring student progress and independent work
- Teacher movement throughout the classroom
- On-task behavior
- Proximity

Directions:

1. Using this chart as a map of the classroom, track the teacher's movement by placing a dot showing the teacher's physical placement during 5 minutes of independent work. Each time the teacher moves, put another dot. Note the time by each dot.
2. Mark in the boxes (student desks) with a '+' to show on-task behavior and a '–' to show off-task behavior for each student.

Teacher Movement Student Participation

Name: ______________________ Date: ____________

Grade/Subject: ______________ Observer: ______________

Use For:

- Monitoring student progress and independent work
- Teacher movement throughout the classroom
- On-task behavior
- Proximity

Directions:

1. Using this chart as a map of the classroom, track the teacher's movement by placing a dot showing the teacher's physical placement during 5 minutes of independent work. Each time the teacher moves, put another dot. Note the time by each dot.
2. Mark in the boxes (student desks) with a '+' to show on-task behavior and a '–' to show off-task behavior for each student.

Cueing Focused Observation Tool

Name: ______________________ Date: __________

Grade/Subject: ______________ Observer: __________

Directions: Use the rating scale to rate performance for both Parts A and B

✓ = Apparent or competent use of Cueing during an evaluation interval

✓+ = Excellent or masterful use of Cueing during an evaluation interval

✓– = Attempted but ineffective use of Cueing during interval

NA or simply leaving an entry blank indicates "not applicable"

Part A: Uses of Cueing. Apply the rating scale to overall performance

	Teacher offers two positive Cues before reminding students of Expectations
	Teacher offers Cues that are clear and understandable
	Teacher uses Cueing with other skills such as Proximity or Signals
	Teacher offers Cues for clarification of Expectations
	Teacher offers Cues for maintenance of social or academic Expectations
	Teacher uses Cueing for redirection of students as needed

Part B: Verbatim Uses of Cueing. Use the spaces below to record specific verbal Cues and to rate the effectiveness of each

Verbatims:	Rating

Observation Notes:

Keepers:

____

____

____

____

Polishers:

____

____

____

____

Cueing
Depth Observation Tool

Observer: ______________________ Grade/Class: ________________

Demo Teacher: ______________________ Date/Time: ______________

Skill Definition: A Cue is a positive verbal reinforcement to assist one or more students to meet social or academic Expectations

Directions: During a 15–minute observation, record statements verbatim into the categories where they seem to fit. Notice that columns for Cueing (on the left) are positive; other kinds of statements may be neutral in tone (middle.) Place negative Cues such as scolding in the right column

Representative Statements Including Cueing					
Cueing Statements (Positive)				**Information, Directions, Questions (Neutral)**	**Scolding (Negative)**
Clarification	**Approval**	**Maintenance**	**Redirection**		

Tally/Frequency: Kinds of Statements	
Kind of Statement	**Apparent Frequency (Tally)**
Clarification Cue	
Maintenance Cue	
Redirection Cue	
Neutral Information	
Negative/Scolding, Sarcasm, etc.	

Cueing Demo Observation Tool

Observer: ______________________ Grade/Class: ________________

Demo Teacher: ______________________ Date/Time: ______________

Skill Definitions: A Cue is a positive verbal reinforcement for any of these purposes:

Clarification of Expectations

Maintenance of expected behavior or activity

Redirection toward correct behavior or activity

Directions: Write examples of your demonstration teacher's Cues in the column labeled "Teacher Action" for the appropriate kind of Cue. For each Cue you enter, describe the "Student Response" in the column to its right

Clarification of Expectations		Maintenance of Expectations		Redirection to Correct Activity	
Teacher Action	Student Response	Teacher Action	Student Response	Teacher Action	Student Response

Teacher Transfer: In my classroom, I want to focus on:

Signals
Focused Observation Tool

Name: ______________________ Date: __________

Grade/Subject: ______________ Observer: __________

Skill Definition: Signals are kinesthetic or other nonverbal indicators from students showing that they understand or are ready for a task.

Directions: Observe for clear directions (Expectations) that include physical indicators (Signals) from children. Use the following rating system:

- ✓ = Strategy is apparent
- ✓+ = Strategy is well done
- ✓– = Strategy is attempted but weak

The teacher . . .

	establishes behavioral Expectations that include a kinesthetic method of response from students
	has students use Signals to verify that they are ready for a task to begin (i.e. put your finger on the first word on the page)
	has students use Signals to engage in direct instruction (e.g., raise your hand if…count on your fingers how many ideas you have. . .)

Observation Notes:

Keepers:

____

____

____

____

____

Polishers:

____

____

____

____

____

Signals
Depth Observation Tool

Name: ______________________ Date: __________

Grade/Subject: ______________ Observer: __________

Directions: 1. Write the teacher direction and students' responses or Signal
2. Write the percentage of students that respond appropriately

Teacher Direction	Kinesthetic Response	%

Observation Notes:

Keepers:

____

____

____

____

Polishers:

____

____

____

____

Signals
Demo Observation Tool

Observer: ______________ Grade/Class: ______________

Demo Teacher: ______________ Date/Time: ______________

Directions: Identify specific uses of Signaling by students that result from the demonstration teacher's direction or Expectation. Then describe students' responses (the Signals they give).

Teacher Direction	Kinesthetic or Nonverbal Response

Teacher Transfer: In my classroom, I want to set and refine this Expectation:

Time Limits
Focused Observation Tool

Name: ______________________ Date: ____________

Grade/Subject: ______________ Observer: ____________

Time Limit: Teacher identifies and communicates specific times for beginning and completing tasks

Directions: Place a rating in the appropriate column

✓ = Competent example of Time Limits
✓+ = Excellent example of Time Limits
✓– = Ineffective example of Time Limits

The teacher . . .

	gives a Time Limit to complete tasks
	gives a Time Limit to begin tasks
	uses Cues to reinforce Time Limits (e.g., "You have 5 seconds to begin 5. . .I see Josh is already started 4. . .Amanda has her pencil moving,. . .")

Observation Notes:

Keepers:

____

____

____

____

____

Polishers:

____

____

____

____

____

Time Limits
Depth Observation Tool

Name: ______________________ Date: ____________

Grade/Subject: ______________ Observer: ____________

Directions:

- Script your teacher's Time Limits in the column labeled "Direction."
- For each Time Limit you enter, note the teacher's support behavior(s).
- Describe the "Student Response" in the column to its right.
- Note the percentage of students who respond appropriately.

Direction That Could Include a Time Limit (Script the Teacher)	Teacher Support (e.g., Proximity, Cueing)	Student Response	%

Observation Notes:

Keepers:

____

____

____

Polishers:

____

____

____

Time Limits Demo Observation Tool

Observer: ____________ Grade/Class: ____________

Demo Teacher: ____________ Date/Time: ____________

Skill Definitions: Teacher identifies and communicates specific times for beginning and completing tasks

Directions: Write examples of your demonstration teacher's Time Limits in the first column. Then, for each Time Limit you enter, note the teacher's support behavior(s) and describe the "Student Response" in the column to its right

Time Limit (Script the Teacher)	Teacher Support Behaviors			Student Response
	Cueing	Proximity	Signals	

Teacher Transfer: In my classroom, I want to set and refine this Expectation:

Time Limits Coaching Tool

Name: ______________________ Date: ____________

Grade/Subject: ______________ Observer: ____________

Time Limit (Script the Teacher)	**Teacher Action** (e.g., Cueing, Proximity, Signals)	**Student Response**	**%**

Tasking Planning Guide

Name: ______________________ Date: __________

Gradet: ________ Topic: ________________________

Directions: Use this tool to plan steps, procedures, and specific questions for upcoming lessons (Teacher DO) as well as the performance you expect (Student DO).

Teacher DO	Student DO
Direct Instruction:	
Guided Practice:	
Independent Practice:	

Tasking
Focused Observation Tool

Name: ______________________ Date: __________

Grade/Subject: ______________ Observer: __________

Time Limit: Teacher identifies and communicates specific times for beginning and completing tasks

Directions: Place a rating in the appropriate column

✓ = Competent example of Tasking
✓+ = Excellent or masterful example of Tasking
✓– = Ineffective attempt at Tasking

The teacher . . .

	uses various methods to keep students engaged during direct instruction (e.g., whisper to your neighbor, note taking guides, white boards)
	engages all students' thinking before one student responds
	provides guided practice including partner and group work
	utilizes active rather than passive engagement

Observation Notes:

Keepers:

____

____

____

____

____

Polishers:

____

____

____

____

____

Tasking Depth Observation Tool

Name: ______________________ Date: __________

Grade/Subject: ______________ Observer: __________

Directions:

1. Observe and record relevant teacher directions.
2. Describe the student response.
3. Estimate and note apparent percentage of students who respond appropriately.

Teacher Direction	Student Response	%

Observation Notes:

Keepers:

____

____

____

____

Polishers:

____

____

____

____

Tasking Demo Observation Tool

Observer: ______________________ Grade/Class: ____________________

Demo Teacher: ______________________ Date/Time: ______________

Directions: Identify and describe specific uses of Tasking by the demonstration teacher. Be sure to enter these as questions or directions under the type of lesson: Direct Instruction, Guided Practice, Independent Practice. Then describe student response for each teacher action.

Direct Instruction		Guided Practice		Independent Practice	
Teacher Action	Student Response	Teacher Action	Student Response	Teacher Action	Student Response

Teacher Transfer: In my classroom, I want to focus on:

Tasking Coaching Tool

Name: ______________________ Date: ____________

Grade/Subject: ______________ Observer: ____________

Directions: Script teacher's questions/directions for response in the appropriate column. During debriefing, coach the teacher to adjust verbiage to move into engagement column

Assessment Questions (Average 5% response)	**Open Questions** (Average 30% – 40% response)	**Engagement Questions** (Average 90% response)

Voice
Focused Observation Tool

Name: ____________________ Date: __________

Grade/Subject: ______________ Observer: __________

Elements of Voice:

Pitch: the highness or lowness of Voice (register)
Tone: the feeling conveyed by the sound of the Voice
Diction: specific word choices
Cadence: movement of Voice upward or downward

Directions: Use the following rating scale

✓ = Competent example of Voice
✓+ = Excellent example of Voice
✓– = Ineffective example at Voice

The teacher . . .

Rating	Techniques for an Effective Voice
	pitches Voice to lower register
	projects Voice to last person in the group
	drops Voice off at the ends of sentences (**cadence**)
	maintains Voice a comfortable pace
	uses an expert **tone** of Voice to project knowledge and authority
	uses a developmentally appropriate **tone** of Voice for the age of her students
	chooses words (**diction**) appropriate to content and grade level

Observation Notes:

Keepers:

____

____

____

____

Polishers:

____

____

____

____

Voice Depth (Interval) Observation Tool

Name: ______________________ Date: ____________

Grade/Subject: ______________ Observer: ____________

Directions: For each interval you observe:

1. Place an star (★) in the box under each Voice PURPOSE and TECHNIQUE that your teacher uses effectively.
2. Put a check (✓–) under each Voice PURPOSE and TECHNIQUE that your teacher missed or didn't use effectively.
3. During your consultation, have your teacher set a goal based upon this data and the Keepers/Polishers.

	Purposes of Voice						Voice Techniques						
	Keep Students' Engagement	Calm Students/ Get Attention	Convey Information/ Directions	Project Authority and Expertise	Communicate Respect and Regard	% Engagement	Pitched at a Low Range.	Drops Off at End of Each Sentence.	Projects to Last Person in Group	Pace Comfortably	Starts Loud; Gets Lower In Volume	Appropriate Expression	Age-Appropriate Language
Interval 1													
Interval 2													
Interval 3													
Interval 4													
Interval 5													
Interval 6													
Interval 7													
Interval 8													
Interval 9													
Interval 10													

Keepers: ____

____

Polishers: ____

____

Teacher Goal: ____

____

Voice Demo Observation Tool

Observer: ____________ Grade/Class: ____________

Demo Teacher: ____________ Date/Time: ____________

Elements of Voice: Voice can be analyzed for Pitch (highness, lowness), Tone (attitude), Diction (word choices), and Cadence (modulation).

Directions: Describe actions by your demonstration teacher that reveal elements of his or her Voice, and enter these descriptions in the center column. Then, for each description, enter your perception of the Voice in the left column, and describe students' responses to those actions and Voice in the right column.

Voice Purpose	Teacher Action (Uses of Voice)	Student Response

Teacher Transfer: In my classroom, I want to:

The Big Eight Engagement Skills for Instruction		
1	**Expectations**	Teacher ensures that students know what to do and when and how to do it.
2	**Attention Prompts**	Teacher uses verbal or visual prompts to focus students' attention for instruction to follow.
3	**Proximity**	Teacher moves purposefully around the classroom for maximum effect.
4	**Cueing**	Teacher uses positive, clear and effective verbal Cues to clarify, maintain, or redirect activity.
5	**Signals**	Teacher uses nonverbal Signals to direct performance, student responses, and other activity.
6	**Time Limits**	Teacher identifies and communicates specific times for beginning and completing tasks.
7	**Tasking**	Teacher focuses and sharpens students' engagement through questioning strategies, purposeful and thought-provoking activities, and other tactics to direct their learning.
8	**Voice**	Teacher uses Voice to maximum effect: pitch in the lower registers, tone geared for situations, diction appropriate to students' age levels, and voice modulation, or cadence, to maintain interest.

REFERENCES

Adams, M. J. (1997). Early Childhood Conference. Dallas, TX: SRA.

Alberto, P. A., & Troutman, A. C. (2006). *Applied behavior analysis for teachers* (7th ed.). Upper Saddle River, NJ: Pearson.

Anderson, V. (1961). *Training the speaking voice*. New York: Oxford Press.

Barkley, S. (2005). Performance Learning, *National Staff Development Conference*. Philadelphia, PA.

Barnes, G., Crowe, E., & Schaefer, B. (2003). *The cost of teacher turnover in five school districts*. Washington, D.C.: National Commission on Teaching and America's Future.

Becker, W. C., & Gersten, R. (1982). A follow-up of Follow Through: The later effects of the Direct Instruction Model on children in fifth and sixth grades. *American Educational Research Journal, 1*(3), 287–307.

Burgoon, J. K., Buller, D. B., & Woodall, W. G. (1989). *Nonverbal communication: The unspoken dialogue*. New York: Harper and Row.

Carnine, D. W., Silbert, J., Kame'enui, E. J., & Tarver, S. G. (2004). *Direct instruction reading*. Upper Saddle River, NJ: Merrill Prentice Hall.

Colvin, G., Sugai, G., Good, R., H.,III, & Lee, Y. (1997). Using active supervision and precorrection to improve transition behaviors in an elementary school. *School Psychology Quarterly, 12*, 344–361.

Cooper, J. O., Heron, T. E., & Heward, W. L. (2007). *Applied behavior analysis*. Upper Saddle River, NJ: Prentice Hall.

Danielson, C. (1996). *Enhancing professional practice: A framework for teaching*. Alexandria, VA: Association for Supervision and Curriculum Development.

Danielson, C., & McGreal, T. L. (2000). *Teacher evaluation to enhance professional practice*. Alexandria VA: Association for Supervision and Curriculum Development.

De Pry, R. L., & Sugai, G. (2002). The effect of active supervision and .pre-correction on minor behavioral incidents in a sixth grade general education classroom. *Journal of Behavioral Education, 11, 255–264.*

DuFour, R., DuFour, B., Eaker, R., & Many, T. (2006). *Learning by doing: A handbook for professional learning communities at work*. Bloomington, IN: Solution Tree (p. 1).

Ferguson, E., & Houghton, S. (1992). The effects of contingent teacher praise, as specified by Canter's Assertive Discipline program, on children's on-task behavior. *Educational studies, 18*(1), 83–93.

Glanz, J., & Neville, R. F. (1997). *Educational supervision: Perspectives, issues and controversies*. Norwood, MA: Christopher-Gordon.

Glickman, C. (2002). *Leadership for learning: How to help teachers succeed*. Alexandria, VA: Association for Supervision and Curriculum Development.

Glickman, C., Gordon, S. P., & Ross-Gordon, J. M. (2004). *SuperVision and instructional leadership: A developmental approach* (6th ed.). Needham Heights, MA: Allyn & Bacon.

Godfrey, S. A., Grisham-Brown, J., & Schuster, J. W. (2003). The effects of three techniques on student participation with preschool children with attending problems. *Education & Treatment of Children, 16*, 255–272.

Granite School District (2005). Domain III: Standards and rubric for learning environment. Salt Lake City, UT: Granite School District.

Granite School District (2006). Granite school district professional growth and evaluation continuum—Selected standards for great beginnings analysis. Salt Lake City, Utah: Granite School District.

Greenwood, C. R., Horton, B. T., & Utley, C. A. (2002). Academic engagement: Current perspectives in research and practice. *School Psychology Review 31*, 328–349.

Greenwood, C. R., Terry, B., Marquis, S., & Walker, D. (1994). Confirming a performance-based instructional model. *School Psychology Review. 23*(4), 652–668.

Gudmundsen, A., Williams, E. J., & Lybbert, R. B. (1996). *You can control your class* (2nd ed.). Novato, CA: Academic Therapy Publications.

Johnson, T. C., Stoner, G., & Green, S. K. (1996). Demonstrating the experimenting society model with classwide behavior management interventions. *School Psychology Review, 25*(2), 199–214.

Joyce, B., & Showers, B. (1984). Transfer of training: The contribution of 'coaching'. In D. Hopkins & M. Wideen (Eds.), *Alternative perspectives on school improvement* (pp. 77–88). London, U.K.: Falmer Press.

Kounin, J. P. (1970). *Discipline and group management in classrooms*. New York: Holt, Rinehart and Winston, Inc.

Lane, K. L., Wehby, J., & Menzies, H. M. (2003). Social skills instruction for students at risk for antisocial behavior: The effects of small-group instruction. *Behavioral Disorders, 28*, 229–248.

Lipton, L., Wellman, B. M., & Humbard, C. (2001). *Mentoring matters: A practical guide to learning-focused relationships*. Sherman, CT: MiraVia, LLC.

Lo, Y., Loe, S. A., & Cartledge, G. (2002). The effects of social skills instruction on the social behaviors of students at risk for emotional or behavioral disorders. *Behavioral Disorders, 27*, 371–385.

Morrison, T. L. (1979). Classroom structure, work involvement, and social climate in elementary school classrooms. *Journal of Educational Psychology, 71*(4), 471–477.

National Board for Professional Teaching Standards (NBPTS). (1987). *The five core propositions*. Arlington, VA: National Board for Professional Teaching Standards.

Sutherland, K. S., Alder, N., & Gunter, P. L. (2003). The effect of varying rates of opportunities to respond to academic requests on the behavior of students with EDB. *Journal of Special Education, 35*(3), 2–8.

Vella, J. (2001). *Taking learning to task: Creative strategies for teaching adults*. San Francisco: Jossey-Bass (p. 3).

Wellman, B., & Lipton, L. (2004). *Data-driven dialogue: A facilitator's guide to collaborative inquiry*. Sherman, CT: MiraVia, LLC.

Winne, P. H., & Butler, D. L. (1994). Student cognition in learning from teaching. In T. Husen & T. Postlewaite (Eds.), *International encyclopaedia of education* (pp. 5738–5745). Oxford, UK: Pergamon.

Yawkey, T. D. (1971). Conditioning independent work behavior in reading with seven year old children in a regular early childhood classroom. *Child Study Journal, 2*(1), 23–34.

Zepeda, S. J. (2007a). *Instructional supervision: Applying tools and concepts* (2nd ed.). Larchmont, NY: Eye on Education.

Zepeda, S. J. (2007b). *The principal as instructional leader: A handbook for supervisors*. Larchmont, NY: Eye on Education.